Companions
in Consciousness

THE **BIBLE** AND THE
NEW AGE MOVEMENT

Companions
in Consciousness

THE BIBLE AND THE
NEW AGE MOVEMENT

/25 1730

Ronald Quillo

Triumph™ Books

Liguori, Missouri

Published by Triumph™ Books
Liguori, Missouri
An Imprint of Liguori Publications

Scriptural citations are taken from the *New Revised Standard Version.*
Copyright © 1989 by the division of Christian Education of the National Council
of the Churches of Christ in the United States of America. Used with permission.

Library of Congress Cataloging-in-Publication Data

Quillo, Ronald.
    Companions in consciousness : the Bible and the New Age movement /
Ronald Quillo. — 1st ed.
        p. cm.
    Includes bibliographical references and index.
    ISBN 0-89243-655-7 : $18.95
    1. New Age Movement.   2. Bible — Criticism, interpretation, etc.
3. Christianity and other religions — New Age movement.   I. Title.
BP605.N48Q55   1994
299'.93 — dc20   93-33422
                                                                                    CIP

Copyright ©1994 by Ronald Quillo
Printed in the United States of America
First Edition

for Julie
my wife and boon companion

Contents

Introduction: What Kind of Companions?

THE AIMS OF THIS BOOK

Companions in Consciousness is written for those who are wondering how the beliefs and practices of the current New Age movement compare with the teachings of the Bible. Some readers already familiar with the New Age may be curious about the degree to which established forms of biblical faith may resemble this modern movement. Other readers at home with such a faith may want a better understanding of the New Age in order to estimate the degree to which it may depart from their own traditional religion.

There are good reasons for trying to examine the Bible and the New Age in light of one another's assumptions, teachings, and practices. The New Age has attracted millions of followers in recent decades and appears to many as an outright challenge to forms of faith nurtured by biblical values. Some New Age enthusiasts may question what traditional faith has to offer a modern age in which so much appears to be changing at exponential rates. On the other hand, many Jews and Christians today have learned of the New Age through the popular media where discussion of relationships between the Bible and the New Age may be minimal or completely ignored. They may also have learned that persons close to them are involved in New Age groups and practices. Questions then arise concerning the appropriateness of such involvement or concerning its compatibility with a faith that is attuned to the Bible.

This book is therefore designed to help readers answer four main questions:

1. What similarities between the Bible and the New Age can be appreciated?
2. How much does biblical faith differ from New Age awareness?
3. How threatening to faith are New Age teachings or practices that appear to depart from biblical instruction or example?
4. What elements that attract people to the New Age can in some way already be found in the Bible or in the practice of a faith rooted in biblical teachings?

Consciousness and Faith

A major feature of the New Age is its pronounced interest in consciousness. The focus is not simply on awareness of facts or of one's surroundings. For the New Age, consciousness involves a person's total being as well as a relationship to all reality. The term *consciousness* encompasses two aspects of awareness: how one understands oneself and one's world, and how one takes responsibility for oneself and one's world. The accent then is on a kind of knowledge, but knowledge that, in the New Age view, is powerful. For knowledge of this kind not only reflects what one knows but also *affects* all one knows, including ourselves and our world. For example, what I think of myself as a worker affects how well I work. Consciousness thus appears as both awareness and influence. My mind affects my world.

To many people today, perhaps especially those who believe in the Bible's teachings on faith and proper living, such claims for consciousness may sound strange because they attribute so much power to the mind. They seem at times to give to consciousness powers that are inappropriate for human beings or that should possibly be reserved for God alone. Therefore the New Age appears in decidedly undesirable light when compared with biblical faith.

Yet the Bible too is interested in consciousness, often in ways that appear to parallel directly the interests of the New Age. A major part of this book is devoted to examining such interests and attempting a verification of the supposed parallels. To the degree that such parallels can be drawn, the Bible and the New Age may rightly be called companions in consciousness. But to say that there are parallels is not to say that the Bible and the New Age always agree. For even close companions may be conscious of their need to disagree on certain points.

In this book I will compare and contrast the kinds of consciousness with which the Bible and the New Age are concerned. I will try to show that there is much more harmony than discord between them. I thus hope to demonstrate that the Bible and the New Age can coexist in a friendly manner, that they are companions in consciousness even though they do not always see eye to eye. Realizing that my project is guided by my personal assumptions and opinions, I leave it to the reader to estimate the extent to which such companionship prevails. Whatever the conclusion, the investigation contains practical teachings that may allow the book to be helpful in refining a personal faith or way of life.

THE MANNER OF PRESENTATION

After outlining some challenges to interpreting the Bible, I review some basic teachings of the New Age movement. Then I examine selected books from the Hebrew and Christian Scriptures in order to estimate how much overlap there may be between them and New Age principles. In concluding I present a summary and my final reflections.

In order to let the Bible speak as much as possible in its own words, I have quoted directly a large number of scriptural verses. Although the citations are selective, my hope is that readers may sense freedom in personally and carefully determining how harmony may prevail between the Bible and the New Age movement.

CHAPTER 1

Looking into the Bible

The Divine Word

Most Jews and Christians know that their Bible, their holy book, is a collection of many different writings. Sacred Scripture is a long series of books or pamphlets that were composed and collected over a period of many centuries, probably from about 1800 B.C.E. (or B.C.) to roughly 130 C.E. (or A.D.). Many different authors were involved in the process, as many titles of the biblical books indicate. To speak of biblical "authors" is not at all to deny the traditional belief that through inspiration God ultimately "authored" this expression of the divine word. Holding to this belief, one can profess that the variety of biblical authors simply witnesses to the various ways by which divine inspiration operated.

The Bible currently exists in at least two distinct forms, one for Jews and one for Christians. The Jewish form contains only those books that Christians call the Old Testament or, more currently, the Hebrew Scripture. The Christian form contains books added after the time of Jesus that are called the New Testament or, more currently, the Christian Scripture. Among Christians themselves at least three forms of the Bible exist, namely one for Roman Catholics, one for Eastern Orthodox Christians, and one for Protestants. The last contains fewer books in the Hebrew Scripture, the ones for which there was no available text in the Hebrew language after the Catholic or Orthodox versions came into common usage. Protestants call these books apocryphal. The differences in versions of the Bible are evidence that editors were involved in assembling Sacred Scripture into distinct collections of books.

BIBLICAL THEOLOGY

The large number of authors and editors of the Bible explains in part why there are so many different points of view expressed in its pages. For example Mark sees and talks about Jesus differently from the way that John does. Not only does one evangelist prefer to emphasize points the other may ignore, but sometimes one assumes that certain things must be said for an audience of which the other might not be aware. Differing viewpoints and distinctive explanations about things pertaining to God can be called distinctive theologies. Such diverse theologies may sometimes be found within a single book, possibly indicating the author or editor might have relied on differing sources or traditions for the material or stories presented in the book.

In spite of this great variety within the Bible, in any of its versions it holds together with a certain amount of remarkable unity. It is as if it were one story or one picture of a particular religion, of a particular way of knowing God and relating to God. It is a portrayal that coheres like a large mosaic on a cathedral wall, each small piece contributing to the beautiful and impressive whole. This shows many readers how much care the editors took in choosing their material and even perhaps in refashioning it a bit for the sake of harmony and order. Certain communities of rabbis, bishops, and others of their faiths canonized the Scriptures, that is they fixed the various versions of the Bible in its final forms. They also took care with the holy word, excluding from it works that were too far-fetched or that were entirely inconsistent with the religious portrait they felt should be preserved for all times.[1]

In general the Bible shows the history, outlook, and practice of a given religious tradition, of a communal heritage marked by devotion to the God of Israel. To the original and more ancient parts of this tradition, the Christian versions of the Bible add the events connected with Jesus and the first generations of the church. The events take place in the Middle East, mostly in the Promised Land or Palestine and in other areas on the Mediterranean Sea, the lands where the influence of ancient Greece and Rome was strong. The culture shaped by such influence is often referred to as Hellenism. People of various sorts, Jew and Gentile, thus participated in telling the story, in instructing for religious practice, and in reflecting on the importance of the way of life to which they felt called.

Each biblical author had a unique way of communicating. So there are many sorts of writings that make up the Bible. Among them are historical accounts, edifying stories or parables, prayers, meditations, moral exhortations, and prophecies. All of these writings coalesce as a primary written witness of the faith that was the source of the Jewish and Christian religions as they are known today.

INTERPRETING BIBLICAL TEACHINGS

The unique heritage of customs and beliefs that make up Judaism and Christianity have developed under the influence of the Bible. This heritage contains much variety in devotions, creeds, liturgies, domestic customs, and forms of recognized leadership or ministry. But the scope of biblically influenced ways of life has seldom appeared to be unlimited. The Bible excludes certain forms of worship from the practice of what it regards as true religion; it also excludes certain practices associated with other religions, cults, or philosophies. With biblical witness as their precedent, Jews and Christians over the centuries have welcomed a wide range of religious expression but also have been careful to point out what is unwelcome or forbidden.

Determining what the Bible welcomes or permits and what it discourages or forbids is not always easy however. Pointing to specific texts can help, but care must be taken to note what exceptions might exist elsewhere. An obvious example of this is the commandment against killing, which, because of other biblical teachings, does not forbid rightful capital punishment. Specific texts are also reversed or amended by later texts. Paul for example teaches his fellow Christians that the traditional Jewish law regarding circumcision does not necessarily apply to them. Determining what the Bible claims is factual can also require care, even if one assumes that the Bible generally speaks literal truths. "I bore you on eagles' wings and brought you to myself" (Ex 19:4)[2] is God's message to

Israel at Mount Sinai. The author hardly appears to mean that this flight should be understood literally, namely as an airborne one. Common sense says that the text is referring metaphorically, or through a figure of speech, to the wondrous way that God rescued the Israelites from captivity in Egypt and helped them flee with ease across the Red Sea. But biblical interpreters and other readers remain divided on how literally the parting of the waters on that occasion should be taken. On each side of the issue, persons find their interpretations appropriate and satisfactory.

So the matter of understanding biblical statements can be even more challenging in other ways. By some current methods of interpretation, certain texts often assumed to be factual are actually exaggerations or imaginative descriptions. In Luke's gospel, the Holy Spirit in the form of a dove clearly descends on Jesus after his baptism by John (Lk 3:21–22). Some readers could say that this scene should not be understood literally but as a fanciful way of depicting Jesus' interior spiritual state. They might find support in this interpretation by referring to Mark, who says of the same incident that the Spirit as dove was something Jesus experienced as "he saw the heavens torn apart" (Mk 1:10). In other words they could suggest the awareness of the heavenly Spirit was something personal and private for Jesus and not an objective experience for bystanders.

An assumption here is that properly interpreting a text requires establishing the intentions of the author. Ancient authors, it is said, frequently give the modern reader the impression that they are writing objective history, namely factual accounts of past incidents, when in fact that may not be entirely true. They may be less interested in factual accuracy and more interested in the impact the story will have on the hearer or reader. Stories can teach moral lessons or inspire virtue whether they are fully factual or not. Examples of these are Jesus' parables. The story of the prodigal son, for example, can teach about God's mercy even if the story is not factual. It is therefore very important, so the claim goes, to know, as far as possible, the author's intentions.

Other interpreters of our day look at the matter differently. They feel that the message of a written text cannot simply stand on its own as a collection of words with meaning in themselves or simply with a meaning explicitly intended by the writer or editor. A message is a link, a form of union or communication between a sender and a receiver. Therefore a lot of what a message communicates has to do with what the receivers expect and what they are capable of receiving. A parent can tell a child, for example, that certain circumstances are desirable; but the child may not make a thorough decision about the implications of the message until she or he attains a certain level of experience, maturity, or intelligence. As Jesus said, "Let anyone with ears to hear listen!" (Mk 4:23)

Current concerns, assumptions, beliefs, or issues are therefore of great importance in understanding the message of a biblical text. They are always part of some individual's or group's interpretive relationship to the Bible.[3] The remark about the Holy Spirit at the scene of Jesus' baptism can be understood in different ways. It can be taken for example as a description of an objective appearance, as a statement regarding Jesus' interior disposition, or as an account of both, depending in great part on what the hearer is ready to accept.

This approach to biblical interpretation helps us understand that reader or hearer readiness affects not only how something is thought to be intended by the author but also how noticeable something is. For example, receiver readiness affects how one thinks about Luke's intentions in writing about the Holy Spirit in the baptism scene. But this readiness can also affect the degree to which the receiver notices whether a change took place in Jesus' consciousness. One group of readers or hearers may perceive little or no such change because they assume that Jesus' knowledge was always complete and could therefore not be supplemented by anything new. Another group may perceive that Jesus grew in religious consciousness because they assume that his human nature allowed for such growth.[4]

Clearly, different interpreters are interested in different things, and this influences what they find in Scripture. The biblical theme of liberation, for example, enjoys more prominence today than in the past since there is heightened concern in our age for the emancipation of blacks, women, and others who are in many ways marginalized or allotted secondary status in society. During the decades in which the Christian Scripture was being written, the early church found in the Hebrew Scripture a number of revelations, especially prophecies, which others could not see. Luke for example quotes Jesus as saying, "Thus it is written, that the Messiah is to suffer and to rise from the dead on the third day" (Lk 24:46). Actually, the Hebrew Scripture to which Jesus was referring contains no direct statement of the kind. Luke however, allows the perspective he has on Jesus to guide his account of the scene so that Jesus may appear as one who throws authoritative light on scriptural texts that to some persons may appear as obscure.[5]

HISTORICAL CRITICISM AND READER RESPONSE CRITICISM

Systematic textual interpretation that gives significant or primary weight to the authoring and editing process is commonly known as historical criticism.[6] Notable or predominant attention given to the assumptions and expectations of the readers or hearers influences a form of systematic textual interpretation called reader response criticism.[7] The first is well established in scholarly works and other writings having an avid interest in biblical interpretation. The extent to which this method leads to taking many texts less than literally varies considerably. The second method is of more recent origin. What is noticeable from the perspectives it offers is that even historical criticism involves regard for readers' assumptions, especially of those readers utilizing the historical-critical method. In other words, what the historical critic concludes regarding the intentions of the ancient authors or editors is often guided by what that critic assumes is credible or acceptable by modern standards.

For example, a historical critic who accepts spiritual or faith healing as a reality may be more inclined to interpret Jesus' healing miracles literally, i.e., to claim that such literalness is what the biblical author intended. It makes sense to such a critic to conclude that the author was stating facts about Jesus' power over disease. On the other hand, a historical critic who doubts the reality of such healing is probably more inclined to be skeptical about an author's intentions in this regard. The critic might find more sense in concluding that the author was speaking figuratively or metaphorically about a change of heart or about spiritual healing in the sense of conversion and renewal.

SUMMARY REGARDING THE BIBLICAL MESSAGE

Reliably and definitively interpreting biblical texts or conclusively stating what the Bible has to say about a particular issue does not appear to be easy. For despite a perceptible unity to the Bible as a whole, there are numerous variables in the Bible itself and a number of inconstancies among the large numbers of believers and other readers of scriptural texts. There is no universal agreement on what constitutes the Bible or on what form of it is normative, namely as the "true" Bible.

Multiple theologies distinguish one biblical book from another or characterize various different traditions within individual books. There are ancient Jewish perspectives represented as well as insights of the ancient Greco-Roman or Hellenistic world. Little agreement prevails on how much of the Bible is historical and how much is composed of other types of writings such as meditations and edifying stories. The Bible sometimes states its own exceptions to rules it has laid down. Biblical authors clearly use metaphor or figures of speech instead of literal descriptions. Different audiences or communities that receive the biblical word have differing assumptions and expectations. Differing groups look for and find different things. Systematic interpretations, like historical criticism and reader response criticism, offer distinctive approaches to understanding scriptural texts.

COMPARING BIBLICAL AND
NEW AGE TEACHINGS

A guiding question of this book is: *To what extent does the Bible harmonize with teachings and practices of the New Age?* In light of the Bible's nature and in light of the principles of interpretation as just discussed, it appears to be a very challenging matter to answer such a question definitively. Answering it presumes certain assumptions about the Bible, about the religion to which it witnesses and which it inspires, and about the New Age itself. Such assumptions guide both analysis of biblical authors' intentions and reader readiness for what these authors appear to be communicating. Much also seems to depend on the impact that the New Age, for better or worse, has made on the reader. A positive impact can be intensified by the attractiveness of New Age principles and practices themselves, or the impact can be diminished by the extent to which one's principles or beliefs appear to forbid agreement with the New Age.

In other words certain values, biases, and preferences are unavoidably present in answering the question. So, quite different answers are possible. Many publications have been dedicated to persuading Christians that the New Age mentality or movement is pernicious and poses a threat to what is sacred and cherished in the Judaeo-Christian tradition.[8] Some of such works are solid and have been well received. Others of them appear as hasty attacks that lack careful analysis of New Age literature, particularly those New Age writings that are of a more scholarly or scientific bent.[9] In the minority at present are writings that, while expressing caution, attempt to show that Christians can tolerate or even welcome certain New Age perspectives and practices.[10]

THE VIEWPOINT OF THIS BOOK

Here an even more accommodating view is taken. My analysis is aimed at showing that:

1. The Bible has much in common with the New Age.
2. Jews and Christians need hardly feel threatened by the New Age.
3. The New Age can actually provide persons with a fresh appreciation of biblical teachings.
4. There are some points on which the Bible and the New Age may never agree.

Among the scholarly materials that have guided my project are works offering various critical approaches to the Bible. My reading of the biblical texts has however been influenced as well by New Age works that, in my view, affect responses to the Bible that may vary from interpretations prevalent in some circles.

My conclusions are offered for the reader's consideration with the hope that the discussions they may encourage will be healthy and contribute to the growth and insight of all parties involved. Other books written within expressly Christian frames of reference have approached the New Age — or practices and teachings associated with it — in a positive, open, or appreciative way. Their authors had their own purposes and their own perspectives.[11] In a world too torn by strife and contention, attempts to foster dialogue and mutual tolerance can contribute to what seems to me are the noblest interests of both the Bible and the New Age movement.

Notes

1. Leo Strauss, "The Beginnings of the Bible and Its Greek Counter-parts" in *Genesis*, ed. Harold Bloom, *Modern Critical Interpretations* (New York: Chelsea, 1986), 39.

2. Biblical citations are from *The New Revised Standard Version* (New York: Oxford, 1989).

3. Kenneth Dauber, "The Bible as Literature: Reading Like the Rabbis," *Semeia* 31 (1985), 31–32.

4. Joseph A. Fitzmyer, *The Gospel according to Luke (I–IX): The Anchor Bible* (Garden City, NY: Doubleday, 1985), 482.

5. Joseph A. Fitzmyer, *The Gospel according to Luke (X–XXIV): The Anchor Bible* (Garden City, NY: Doubleday, 1985), 1558, 1565–67, 1581–84.

6. Edgar Krentz, *The Historical-Critical Method* (Philadelphia: Fortress, 1975).

7. Edgar V. McKnight, *Post-modern Use of the Bible: The Emergence of Reader-oriented Criticism* (Nashville: Abingdon, 1988), 167–96.

8. For example: Russell and Marjorie Lee Chandler, "The Magnet of New Age Mysticism," *Columbia* (July 1990), 6–8; Douglas R. Groothuis, *Unmasking the New Age* (Downers Grove, IL: InterVarsity, 1986); Frank E. Peretti, *This Present Darkness* (Westchester, IL: Crossway, 1986); Ralph Rath, *The New Age: A Christian Critique* (South Bend, IN: Greenlawn, 1990); Kerry D. McRoberts, *New Age or Old Lie?* (Peabody, MA: Hendrickson, 1989); *Not Necessarily the New Age: Critical Essays*, ed. Robert Basil, (Buffalo, NY: Prometheus, 1988).

9. Lowell D. Streiker, *New Age Comes to Main Street: A Non-Hysterical Survey of the New Age Movement* (Nashville: Abingdon, 1990), 23.

10. For example: Loren Wilkinson, "New Age, New Consciousness and the New Creation," in *Tending the Garden: Essays on the Gospel and the Earth*, ed. Wesley Granberg-Michaelson (Grand Rapids, MI: Eerdmans, 1986), 6–29; Ted Peters, *The Cosmic Self: A Penetrating Look at Today's New Age Movements* (San Francisco: Harper, 1991).

11. For example: Ken Carey, *Terra Christa: The Global Spiritual Awakening* (Kansas City: Uni-Sun, 1985); Matthew Fox, *The Coming of the Cosmic*

Christ: The Healing of Mother and the Birth of a Global Renaissance (San Francisco: Harper, 1988); Matthew Fox, *Creation Spirituality: Liberating Gifts for the Peoples of the Earth* (San Francisco: Harper, 1991); John J. Heaney, *The Sacred and the Psychic: Parapsychology and Christian Theology* (New York: Paulist, 1984); John Rossner, *In Search of the Primordial Tradition and the Cosmic Christ* (St. Paul, MN: Llewellyn, 1989); Lowell D. Streiker, *New Age Comes to Main Street*; David Toolan, *Facing West from California's Shores: A Jesuit's Journey into New Age Consciousness* (New York: Crossroad, 1987); William Warch, *The New Thought Christian* (Marina del Rey, CA: DeVorss, 1977).

CHAPTER 2

Is the New Age New?

OLD AND NEW

One may rightly question the newness of the New Age. Many of its features are centuries-old or have their roots in ancient philosophies and religions of both the West and East. Below I list and explain eleven general features of the New Age. Its relationship to historical or established theories and practice will be mentioned there as occasions arise. From another perspective however, the New Age is appropriately named. Its elements have in recent decades been taking on new widespread intensity and appear as part of a changing consciousness and sense of responsibility in our time.

The New Age is an international movement involving a large number of views, practices, and programs, an enormous catalogue of items[1] that are difficult to classify under a single heading. They include the work of many types of persons in a variety of fields. Taking part are — besides occultists and charismatic media personalities — established scholars in such fields as physics, psychology, anthropology, biology, physiology, ecology, philosophy, and religious studies.

As I see it, the common thread of the New Age is a renewed and intensified enthusiasm for the nonempirical or spiritual dimensions of reality insofar as they are thought to hold all reality in relatedness, unity, and a dynamic movement toward improvement. This thread or common denominator is part of a late twentieth-century delight in the unity by which all things anticipate perfection or grow toward it physically and spiritually. Such enthusiasm or interest has been somewhat dampened in cultures or soci-

27

eties that, like our own, have been significantly touched by the Enlightenment and the rise of the empirical sciences. The Enlightenment was an eighteenth-century movement in which human reason and intelligence became newly appreciated as ways to test or move beyond unfounded or superstitious beliefs. The empirical sciences are those in which the measurable and tangible play a significant role in performing and repeating experiments to verify theories and conclusions.

The age of the Enlightenment and the environment of the modern sciences have had, sometimes contrary to their initial intentions, an enormous influence on how we look at the world today. In other words reason, logic, and tangible procedures often appear to be more reliable and valuable than faith. From this perspective intuition and the acceptance of the nonempirical or spiritual is difficult, if not unlikely.

THE NEW AGE AND GOD

I must grant that the domain of the nonempirical is not necessarily identical with the divine as traditionally understood within Judaism and Christianity, namely as characterized by absolute transcendence. By this I mean that there are some things (for example electronic waves, psychic energies, or spirits) that, it is claimed, belong to an order beyond the senses but which Jews and Christians would not say are the same as their God. For their tradition God is one who, while close to all and redemptively loving, transcends or reigns absolutely distinct from all as creation's originator and supreme orderer. For Christians this God is uniquely revealed through the identity and mission of Jesus Christ. Such understanding of God is part of what makes interests of the New Age suspect to many of those whose faith is rooted in biblical teachings. To them the New Age may appear to be dealing in realities or in a dimension of being not at all related to their God. From this perspective the interests of the New Age seem nearly valueless if not outrightly ungodly.

Yet the New Age believes in a nonempirical dimension that connects all humanity. It sees this connection and talks about it in various ways. Indeed it draws on Eastern and Western traditions that sometimes appear outlandish in a Judaeo-Christian society. But it also holds in high esteem thinkers who are familiar with biblical teachings and who, out of scholarly sensitivity or personal faith in the Bible's God, associate the nonempirical, as they see it, with the divine.

The psychologist Carl Jung for example finds that beyond the world of the ego or ordinary consciousness there are the personal unconscious and a "collective unconscious" in which God or the divine is eminently active.[2] This means, briefly, that there are deeper layers to ourselves of which we have only indirect knowledge. These aspects of us influence how we act in life and how we feel about it. They are in a certain way molded by our upbringing and life experiences. But how we were raised and what we experience in our world is also influenced by the spiritual bond that all persons enjoy with one another. An essential part of our lives is or can be guided, both as individuals and societies, by the divine element that is part of these deeper layers. For Jung this divine element is the one who is commonly called God.

Looking at life from a different viewpoint, the eminent paleontologist and theologian Pierre Teilhard de Chardin spoke of a kind of evolving superconsciousness or "noosphere" that is shaping humanity in the image of Christ.[3] By this he meant in essence that all humans are growing closer to one another through the knowledge and love that they can share and deepen through the power of God who, incarnate in Jesus Christ, ultimately binds them together.

That proponents of the New Age see a link between their interests and the interests of biblical faith[4] does not necessarily mean that all those whose faith is inspired by the Bible will see that link as well. Jews and Christians may not all agree, in other words, that the divine or transcendent as the New Age understands it is in any way, large or small, the same as the Bible's God. In studying both the Bible and numerous New Age publications, I have concluded however that the link is there. I know that to many readers this will remain a debatable if not deniable conclusion. I offer my evidence for it, then, not as definitive but as worth considering.

Christians, Jews, and other believers who accept that their God is to some degree active and knowable outside their own traditions will have an easier time with my argumentation than those who believe that authentic religiousness is absolutely limited to forms of faith connected with the Bible. Moderate and liberal circles in Judaism and Protestant Christianity see outside their faiths some presence and benefits of divine influence in varying degrees. Roman Catholic Christianity holds by official teaching that God can be known and the divine presence can be enjoyed outside of Christian faith, though by Christian perspectives incompletely. Not all Jews and Christians appear to take such positions however. The association of the New Age with other forms of faith or perception of the divine — whether ancient, modern, Eastern, or Western — may thus help or hinder one's sense of how much the New Age involves the divine element or the God regarded by biblical faith as true.

FINDING LINKS BETWEEN THE BIBLE AND THE NEW AGE

In my view many ideas and practices that the New Age speaks of are also appreciated in the Judaeo-Christian tradition, but according to this tradition's modes of expression. Much of this expression — the tradition's language, terminology, symbols, images, etc. — comes from the Bible. My book is therefore about examining how strong the linkage is and what its limits might be. I am speaking here of the most typical features or, by common standards, the most respectable face of the New Age movement. Any complex movement, even if religious, can have its fringe groups that distort it and even shape it to look devilish. Such as these I do not regard as authentically New Age and therefore exclude them from my considerations. Everything I say about the New Age will be about the overwhelming majority of those who are identified with it and are dedicated to improving the human condition and life in our world. Like most people, New Agers must struggle. They have much room for improvement and maturation.[5] They make mistakes and have regrets. But they also have hope, a dream of attaining something quite wonderful, a destiny to be sought in joy and pain.

PRINCIPLES OF THE NEW AGE

What therefore can the New Age movement be said to be, and how new is it? Despite the astounding variety of theories and practices associated with the New Age, certain key principles can be observed as general characteristics. Not all New Agers may hold to each of the principles equally, nor does my list of principles consider everything associated with the New Age. As in many movements or groups, there is variety in individual members' priorities regarding particular beliefs or practices. But the generalized features of the New Age as listed here can provide a reasonable and workable basis on which to compare this movement with teachings of the Bible.

The literature that I use throughout the book to depict the New Age is from many disciplines or areas of study. But all of these works, in my view and that of others who share the vision called New Age, partake to some significant degree in representing common interests. I find it valuable to depict the New Age according to eleven principles held by its proponents, though at times in quite varying ways. The mosaic emerging from this eleven-point depiction thus constitutes less a unified vision and more a coherent representation of compatible and mutually supporting perspectives.

1. Everything is divine, including human consciousness.

There are philosophers and theologians who would say that this principle is the basis of a pantheistic metaphysics. When someone attempts to account for the ultimate constitution of reality or to depict methodologically how reality exists in its most basic or essential form, that person is employing metaphysics. If such a method includes the idea that divine being is the essence of all reality — and amounts to saying that everything is God — the metaphysics employed is said to be a pantheistic one. Metaphysics of this kind has much in common with the teachings of Hinduism, the ancient and established religion of India.

Hinduism and other religions of the East are also called monistic, which means they are belief systems that think of all reality as essentially one; the differences that appear to exist among things and persons are said to be merely illusions. Personal and spiritual growth in these religions is regarded as a process by which one learns to experience and appreciate the oneness of all rather than the apparent differences or separations. Growing in this way is believed to be the basis of personal peace and of harmony between all persons and other reality.

Much in the New Age view of our world depends on this first principle commonly regarded as pantheistic or monistic. Since by it all is regarded as God, all is of infinitely sublime essence and destiny. This means that all reality is basically the noblest sort of being and is moving toward a most wonderful future in accord with its sublime nature; suffering and evil, which are insubstantial though persistent, will eventually lose all delusive power.

Proponents of New Thought, one of the numerous historical roots of the New Age,[6] find inspiration in such a principle and can say that "God is invisible intelligence, energy and love,"[7] meaning that this energy and love suffuses and constitutes everything, literally the whole universe. Human awareness then would have to be thought of as part of this universal power. Thus the New Age can accept with enthusiasm the research and theories of current physics that support a view that below the everyday, empirical, or objective world is a layer or stratum of reality in which everything is held together in an unbroken wholeness.[8] In this stratum everyday reality is implicate or enfolded in some orderly way so that in ordinary experience reality takes the form of an orderly unfolding of events and truths. It is however the implicate order that is basic to reality, not the explicate or everyday order. And, since experience is a part of the unfolding of reality, consciousness appears as a factor of the fundamental implicate order, which itself may have many levels.[9]

Employing Christian terms but without an abandonment of monistic assumptions, certain New Age forms of spirituality call human consciousness *what Christ is* as a point of divine consciousness. This point is the Christ in each human being[10] or is each human being endowed with the "Christ Mind" inspired by the Holy Spirit.[11] This is a way of saying that human consciousness is not in fact human distinct from the divine but is actually part of the one divine mind or being. Human consciousness is thus said to be directed, with all else, toward fulfillment beyond what seems to be of immediate concern, beyond what appears as ephemeral and transitory. Finding happiness or blessedness means moving toward what we essentially are, namely God, or developing toward oneness in the unity of all.[12] From this New Age perspective then, the nonempirical or spiritual is necessarily within the realm of the divine, as is all other reality, including the everyday or empirical.

2. Truth is constituted from within.

Westerners have generally been taught that knowing the truth means opening oneself, or one's mind, to reality or facts insofar as they are available to or outside the self or mind. Thought of in this way, truth about a house, for example, might be that it has so many rooms; or truth about the self is that it knows. The self or mind is thus thought to connect with or correspond with something different from itself (for example, with the house) or at least with something known to itself (for example, with the mind as thought of by itself). From a New Age perspective the division assumed here between mind (or subject) and the reality known (or object) is not entirely warranted. The New Age would also say that the connections or correspondences between subjects and objects in the typical Western idea of truth is needlessly complicated or not in accord with the simpler contours of knowing and awareness. For truth and consciousness appear as more one than divided.

The New Age sees all reality, including the operations of truth, as identical with what eminently is, namely the divine or one reality. Truth then is nothing more than this one or divine as manifested, that is insofar as it is appearing within or to a knowing subject. From this perspective to know a house has so many rooms is not to connect or correspond as a subject with a building outside of myself but simply to be aware that I am aware of a reality, in this case a house, with which I am one. The house and I are thus one in reality or part of one another; there is no real division between me and the house I know, although it may seem that way.[13]

Another way to understand this is to reflect on the relationship of realization and reality. Here one can see that reality is consistently linked with our descriptions of it. Thus the greatest truths, even ones connected with the divine or God, are enmeshed in descriptions that knowing persons formulate and are thus disclosed in rather arbitrary or changeable systems of communication. The use of metaphors or symbols in such a system helps us become aware that what speaks to one person, or what is true for one person, may not be true for another, at least not in the same way.[14] To me the house may be a "palace." To you it may be a "shack." In a real sense each of us makes the house what it is, or what is true about it for each of us.

This kind of thinking about truth did not begin with the New Age but is quite ancient in both the East and West. During the last few centuries, something akin to such thought has been approached in the transcendental or idealist traditions of Western philosophy.

The New Age contributes to claims that metaphysics or theory of being crosses over into epistemology or theory of knowledge. Metaphysics is also said to cross over into hermeneutics or theory of interpretation since what I find someone or some text saying is intimately related to how I think truth is found or constituted. Where subjectivity and objectivity are thought to merge, as they do according the principle that truth is constituted from within, truth is not certitude of what is apparent to or knowable for a subject but is the sureness of being one with all else within the single divine reality.[15]

For the New Age then, truth is not something I merely deduce or discover but something that happens when I become sure of myself or aware of the one reality, especially when this occurs in a special and undisturbed way. Truth is something of a change from merely being what I ordinarily seem to be to knowing what I surely am in the entire scope of things. Because of a unity apparent at a deeper level of reality, certain contemporary physicists highly respected by the New Age can regard human consciousness as open to the awareness of all reality. Like a hologram (a special photograph in which each part contains the image of the whole) the mind appears as a reflection of all things.[16] Recent neuroscience has suggested that the human brain itself is a hologram that relates to all things because the universe itself is holographic.[17] If truth is constituted from within, says the New Age, then the mind is not just receptive to the totality but also has an influence on it.

This kind of awareness in the larger totality of reality can suitably be called enlightenment.[18] One of the most famous instances of enlightenment — as awareness of a larger unity that escapes everyday knowledge — is that of Siddhartha Gautama, who founded the Buddhist religion more than 2500 years ago. In Buddhism it is not certitude but enlightenment that is desired above all else.

Wanting certitude leaves the subject passive to the object or can make the subject a victim of circumstances. Truth in the New Age view leaves the world or object passive to the enlightened subject and thus under the subject's ennobling influence.[19] For example, thought about oneself as healthy is believed to influence positively one's health.[20] Thoughts about peace are likewise believed to influence the attainment of peace. In this sense subjectivity can be determinative of what is true and thus real, even in the physical world.[21] How we look at things determines what we find. Common experiences of this occur for the optimist who finds more good in life than bad, while the pessimist finds more reason to bemoan life than to rejoice in it.

3. Growth in consciousness or overcoming faulty consciousness is the key to blissful living and the immediate goal of all enlightened persons.

When we do not know the truth, we are at odds with reality. Since reality is one, says the New Age, to be at odds with it is to be at odds with ourselves. Thus we feel disorder and uneasiness; our lives can be wanting in peace and contentment. So interruptions of truth in our lives can breed a plaguing dissonance. This kind of disharmony results in ignorance of various sorts: factual ignorance or obliviousness regarding our predicament or the state of matters that could concern us; theoretical ignorance or an opportunity lost for grasping ideas or strategies; and moral ignorance or missed occasions for properly determining right and wrong. Uninformed, dull, and corrupt persons can exemplify these various categories of ignorance. But the dissonance bred by interruptions of truth also results in pain of various sorts: physical pain or bodily suffering; emotional pain or distress coupled with bothersome feelings; and mental pain or psychological anguish in various forms.[22] Sick, sorrowing, and unstable persons might exemplify affliction by these various sorts of pain.

Faulty identification with truth can, according to New Age belief, be due to various factors. Perhaps one of the greatest sources of ignorance and pain is the habit of attributing great importance to that which is not as important as it appears. Undue attachments to possessions or persons are obvious examples of falsely rating what we think are essential ingredients in our lives. The New Age holds that attachments of this sort distract us from the ultimate unity of all reality because things like needless possessions and harmful relationships blind us to the higher truth of our oneness with the divine or because such things, as only aspects, monistically speaking, of the one reality do not really exist in themselves at all.[23]

Another source of ignorance and pain is the stubborn adherence to concepts or conclusions that likewise distract from those that are more closely linked with the greater whole and thus engender greater happiness.[24] Determination that one *must* achieve certain goals or attain so much power in order to be happy is an example of an attitude that can hinder authentic or truly valuable ways of attaining happiness. Determination of this kind can be a needless detour or blind alley on the way to personal and lasting fullness of being. So can inflexible determination of what is good for others, especially for significant others or those for whom one is responsible. Untruth here can backlash into retaliation or broken relationships.

The connection of untruth with misery is ancient and finds modern expression in more than the New Age. Hinduism has taught for centuries that *maya*, the deceptive collection of material and transitory realities, are no more than illusions. The only true being according to this religion is the single divine reality called *Brahman*. Gnosticism is a philosophy and way of life with probable origins in the first century. Here it was believed that salvation is intrinsically linked with the knowledge of one's place in the divine, immaterial world; any other knowledge was construed to be negligible or false.

Of recent origin in the world of modern psychology is cognitive therapy, a methodology whose assumptions are much appreciated by the New Age. For here thoughts or states of mind are held to be intimately linked with physical and psychological health.[25] Cognitive therapy aims to help patients overcome debilitating effects of distorted cognitions or thoughts. Convictions regarding one's identity or achievements can harm both the body and psyche. For example, one can be persuaded that one will "have to be married" before a certain age or that one "will never finish" a task thought to be important. Such convictions can eat at one's soul if they are not replaced with more helpful expectations, hopes that can in fact free one to attain the goals toward which the harmful thoughts were inappropriately directed. Religions, philosophies, or scientific procedures that, ancient or modern, help persons develop beyond constraining knowledge and into fuller truth are all related to the New Age principle of attaining bliss through growth to higher consciousness.

4. Death leads to reincarnation.

According to the New Age, higher consciousness and thus blissful salvation are usually the end of a lengthy process involving continued dedication, rededication, multiple trials and errors, and relentless endurance. The pull of unreality seems too strong, and the temptation to succumb to illusions' tricks seems too great for it to be otherwise. Notable progress can indeed be made, and advances can be observed within relatively short and manageable periods. One can reasonably hope to experience successes like these.

But higher consciousness in its *ultimate form* means totally untarnished identity with reality's truth. A goal like this, then, is not likely achieved in short order and, says the New Age, may not even be accomplished over a single long lifetime.[26] The idea is not that overcoming faulty consciousness usually involves a purification or purgation in a single spiritual state sometime after death. Something like the latter idea is part of the Roman Catholic and Eastern Orthodox doctrine of purgatory. Rather, the New Age view is that multiple attempts within a succession of physical lives are usually requisite until one enjoys undistorted wholeness and the fullness of being.[27] Here the New Age enjoys solidarity with the age-old doctrine that is important in two great world religions,

Hinduism and Buddhism. According to their beliefs, the soul or spirit, the essence of the individualized person, migrates from life to life and body to body until the ultimate state of higher consciousness is reached. The speed with which the process occurs, both within an individual life and over a succession of lives, is influenced by the morality and responsibility exhibited by the person in the various lifetimes. Choices for good enrich one's life and thus speed one toward the desired identity of consciousness with truth. Choices for evil, ignorance, or irresponsibility retard the process and may even, if only temporarily, reverse it. The journey toward truth is thus regarded as an undertaking of the highest importance. No task is worthier of one's undivided attention.

5. There are numerous valid paths to divinity.

Personal growth within the divine unity requires some kind of methodology or praxis. One must *do something*, sometimes following a pattern or routine. Such practice can vary from individual to individual and be very personal and unique. Private practice in this area is possible, says the New Age, even if one does not appear to be expressly religious or pious. But formal, established religions are widespread. And they are, the New Age also agrees, probably the most common systems that nurture, guide, and critique development in consciousness and bliss.[28]

Other meaning systems such as those provided by philosophy, psychology, or politics do so as well. According to their qualities and the extent of individual involvement in them, they and the various religions do so to greater or lesser degrees. In other words, even if one methodology is supposedly inferior to another, some people go about their tasks more dedicatedly or efficiently and thus achieve more than less energetic practitioners of supposedly better systems.

Any such system however, whether expressly religious or otherwise, to the extent that it is conducive to greater bliss and heightened consciousness, is said to be true and viable. To someone led by New Age principles, this need not mean that the personal path to heightened consciousness must be a form of syncretism or some unusual and possibly shallow combination of elements from several religions or philosophies. It may in fact mean appreciating New

Age principles, practicing wholeheartedly a single traditional religion or methodology, and being aware of many other peoples' ways of proceeding according to their own traditions or choices. For the New Age such acceptance of others becomes a safeguard against narrowness, rigidity, and superficiality.[29]

The New Age then, like Eastern religions typically, including Hinduism and Buddhism, is characterized by profound tolerance for innumerable edifying religions[30] and meaning systems. Western religions like Judaism, Christianity, and Islam are traditionally not as tolerant. In each are found claims to be the best religion or even the only true one. The present times have been called pluralistic since increasing numbers of people appear to realize the advantages of accepting a plurality of respectable philosophies, or of accepting various persons' ways of living and attaining happiness. The New Age shares this mentality and is naturally at home with pluralism.

6. The attainment of bliss involves concern for the good of all.

Turning within for truth or following the teachings of a great religious or philosophical teacher commonly exposes one to the mutuality and relatedness of human beings, one with another. That is, we discover that we are all brothers and sisters influencing one another in various ways. Webs or systems of interdependence are visible historically and culturally. We are bred into ways of speaking and relating to one another, and soon we discover that we are seldom loners in attaining health, sustenance, or well-being. We look to one another for basic needs, for expressions of beauty such as art and music that make life more pleasant, and for the security and love that so affect our identities and values. The external or cultural expressions of interdependence are, says the New Age, manifestations of the deeper unity of humanity in the greater whole, the universal and spiritual bond by which all reality is interrelated in a dynamic way.[31] The good of one of us is associated with the good of others.[32]

Persons have enormous influence on one another, for better or worse. All of us therefore are faced with tremendous responsibilities that are morally or ethically binding. Dedication to common growth and happiness is thus intrinsic to individual growth.[33]

One cannot look out for oneself without looking out for others. The New Age, like the great religions of the world, and even like the admirable elements of some philosophical or social systems, aspires by its very essence to altruism or seeking the good of others. In its essence, in the unity of all things, the New Age strives to live according to an ideal of limitless love extended without fear; it strives to live in humble service that seeks the good of all.[34]

7. Health means wholeness and unity of body, mind, and spirit.

Bodily well-being or good health is something obviously biological but not just that. Wellness of body in the New Age view manifests wholesome growth within the whole of being. Health is a quality of every dimension of one's existence and is caught up in every dimension of reality generally, both the empirical and non-empirical or the physical and spiritual.[35] Since, in its essential unity with the divine, all of being is good, being is essentially salubrious. By its very nature in other words, being in its oneness stimulates or cultivates health. According to the New Age, we can resist being's health-giving power by negativity, especially negative thoughts.

The body's health is thus connected with higher consciousness, namely with the healthy or healing mind as it progresses in truth. This does not appear to mean that an enlightened or spiritually maturing mind *always* comes to expression in a whole or healthy body, since parts of the mind may still require growth. However the link between body and mind is there.

Body and mind moreover, as linked to the self in its inherent oneness with the divine, are bound with the human spirit. One's physical part, the body, along with one's mental or psychological part, the mind, are joined with the soul or spirit, that deepest and most mysterious part of oneself where one's personal identity and individuality are given their unique stamp for a given time in human history according to the determinations of the divine order. Through the spirit, the divine defines who one is and in what ways one may develop and find bliss. Body, mind, and spirit are thus mutually dependent during a given historical lifetime, the progressing heartiness or enfeeblement of one influencing the heartiness or enfeeblement of the others.[36]

In other words, the condition of one's body, mind, *or* spirit can influence for better or worse the condition of the other two. Even as positive thoughts of one's mind can stimulate in one's spirit an intensified closeness to the divine and can nurture the health of one's body, so either the spirit or body can contribute to the mind's enrichment, as may be the case when physical or spiritual conditioning influences positive attitudes or heightened insights. In attaining their individual wholeness, the three — body, mind, and spirit — can move toward fullness and integration, one with the others.[37] Attentive activities in all three areas — say through diet and exercise, study and reflection, or meditation and prayer — can thus become equally important.

This integrative approach to health is frequently termed holistic. In drawing on the principles and procedures of holistic health and healing, the New Age joins forces with the various forms of healing that have been practiced over the centuries.[38] Faith healing, which depends on the effects of the renewed spirit on the health of the body, predates the beginning of the Common Era or time of Jesus Christ and was known in both the ancient Jewish and Hellenistic worlds. Shamanism is the long-standing traditional form of healing that has prevailed among so-called primitive peoples. Often it has acquired a negative reputation, being identified with malicious forms of witchery. But it is being increasingly studied in recent times because of its holistic approach to healing. In its best and most common form it involves the artistry and skills of the healer or shaman who combines the use of natural medicines with refined techniques of psychological influence and spiritual power.[39] Increasingly alert to the potential of holistic health, shamanistic healing, and New Age awareness, modern medicine observes that hope awakened through thought, images, or suggestion has power to heal a wide variety of disorders or illnesses.[40]

8. The unity of all requires closeness to and respect for nature.

The linkages of individuals with others, along with the linkages of body, mind, and spirit, manifest the truth of the oneness of all. As such these linkages parallel and complement a global linkage of individuals and societies with the planet's — if not the universe's — natural attributes and processes. In professing such interconnectedness, the New Age agrees with what is called ecological or constructive postmodernism, a contemporary view whereby substantive meaning in life is found through a perception of the deeper or fundamental unity of all things.[41] The New Age finds scientific support for this in modern theory where the earth is regarded as one living entity, a single system of organisms that reflects life at all levels of the planet's ecology.[42] If all is one, then the oneness of all must include humanity's closeness and harmony with all of nature.[43]

But we enjoy our relationship with nature in many ways. We can turn to it for the food it spontaneously provides when we gather wild berries or nuts, when we camp and take in the beauty of forests and hills, or when we relax on a weekend of fishing. But we also turn to nature in more assertive ways when we manipulate it through such industries as agriculture, mining, or lumbering. Such bending of nature to our purposes can easily become aggression if nature is abused or deprived of its innate capacities to regenerate healthily or to fulfill its place in the harmonious order of all creation. Such aggression is thus a kind of irreverence[44] that violates ourselves as well as nature.[45] The New Age points to pollution of our soil, air, and water as examples of such irreverence.

Influence over or perfection of nature through human creative intervention must be guided, says the New Age, by the truth of personal wholeness and higher consciousness. These work in tandem with the truth determinable within nature itself, which has an inherent disposition toward perfection within the greater order of matter, spirit, and the divine.[46] The natural sciences help us understand much about nature's truths and its potential for self-healing. Such sciences should be eminently respected. But enlightened consciousness must also learn to listen in a sensitive and intuitive way to nature.[47] Ecological awareness at its deepest level is profoundly spiritual.[48] Every person, whether a dweller of the city or the country, can find a way to let nature speak to the heart. Each person can find a way to exhibit respect for nature and its needs. The New Age thus finds environmental concerns essential to its interests in the well-being of all.[49]

Respect for nature even extends to interest in healing and nurturing agents such as herbs, natural essences, and crystals, all of which may have been less disturbed by technologies that may mar nature's pristine and subtle energies. Crystals, which have been respected by numerous cultures worldwide and throughout history, are felt to have a special structure that keeps them in a certain communion with nature at many levels.[50] Such sensitivity to natural elements reveals how intimacy with the powers of nature comes back upon the individual and breeds greater sensitivity to the holistic unity in which all persons dwell.

9. We need to trust intuition, imagination, and feeling.

The wholeness of body, mind, and spirit, the wholeness facilitated through growth in consciousness, involves the developing person or self in its unity with all. This self stands in contrast with the individual insofar as she or he is what may be called an ego. The self is that dimension of a person insofar as she or he is, through heightened consciousness and harmonious relationships, in touch with the fullness of being.[51] The ego is the dimension of the person that is more in tune with realities — especially with concrete or empirical objects — insofar as they distract from truth and remain as what Hindus call *maya* or illusion.

More in the grips of distracting objects than the self enjoying truth, the ego in recent ages has been drawn into notable objectivity, that is, it has become an object of attention in itself, sometimes for good, but often for ill. For the last few hundred years education and other influences of Western culture have been significantly influenced by what can be called a Newtonian view of reality. The New Age likes to point out that the Newtonian view nurtures empirical sciences and positivist mentalities. In other words, the Newtonian outlook on life puts much stock in the work of empirical or natural sciences (such as physics, chemistry, and biology) and stresses the importance of what in our experience is tangible, measurable, and generally knowable through the five senses.

It is difficult to imagine our world without the modern sciences. For common sense and a vast amount of evidence point to the good these sciences have done, bringing advances in technology, progress in medicine, and products that contribute to life's pleasures. Whatever corrective such advances have been to excesses or ignorance of the past, and whatever marvels and wonders they have introduced for improving our world, the New Age feels that they stand today in need of balancing. For our knowledge of the world appears to depend as well on the imagination and unconscious to interpret and organize what we perceive,[52] as when we assess the greatness of something far away even though it looks small. So in fact science itself in most recent times no longer professes to offer exact descriptions of reality, only approximate ones[53] where imagination plays an important part. Our approach to life and truth can be too much influenced by what we think is merely measurable, linear, empirical, or subject to exact logic and calculation.

Excess of this modern kind is frequently linked with the part of the brain that is said to be more rational or scientific. Such "left brain" activity needs the balance of affect and intuition, of feeling and instinctual insight. A person can draw on such powers of human nature rather than on logic or concrete investigation to determine what is going on or what the essence of an issue might be. Anyone who has done so is naturally sensitive to the value of intuition and feeling, even though she or he might not know that in such cases another part of the brain is said to be predominantly active.

These "right brain" dispositions are often nurtured or assisted in their operations through individual imagery provided by the unconscious and expressed in such forms as dreams or artistry.[54] Below the surface of us all, say many psychologists, lies the unconscious domain that is very creative and that is a storehouse of wisdom as well as a place where most of our problems and struggles have their root. Dreams can put us in contact with this domain,[55] or it can come to light through images we create, say in drawing pictures or writing poetry. It can also come to light or give us guidance when we respond to images others create, as when we are moved to insight by a poem or find comfort in a particular religious or artistic symbol. "Right brain" dispositions may similarly be nurtured by cultural imagery provided by sages and storytellers. Fables, fairy tales, and myths usually have morals or wise directives that can profoundly influence decisions we make and courses we pursue. Whether coming in sleep or during group assemblies, the images that emerge from individuals and peoples are a rich resource for helping us be more intuitive or affective.

Thus the New Age finds great interest in the psychology of the unconscious, in the mythologies of all ages and peoples, and in the more recent advances of the natural sciences that are discovering that symbol, suggestion, and paradox[56] — to which the "right brain," more than the "left," appears to be more receptive — are at times the most suitable ways to express realities that defy purely empirical or positivist understanding.[57] This latter understanding creates only discriminations and certitude. The new sciences, like the new physics, for example, foster a more inclusive awareness of the unity of all.[58]

10. We need to trust paranormal phenomena.

Heightened interest in "right brain" activity has brought with it renewed sensitivity to phenomena that in the past were much more acceptable and welcome. Practices like fortune-telling, astrology, spiritualism, and magic in those days fit into the expectations and beliefs of people in various cultures. Many modern persons who have been substantially influenced by a Newtonian view of reality are ill-receptive to things that do not appear to be scientifically verifiable. These practices or skills belong to the world of ESP or extrasensory perception.

Some contemporary physicists are suggesting that such extraordinary phenomena operate on the basis of the unity of the mind with all reality at its deeper unifying level.[59] With these phenomena there is indeed room for much fraud and other unethical practice. The New Age however is open to and even enthusiastic about the proper use of certain phenomena that appear to fit into its practice of relating positively to the nonempirical. Such phenomena include clairvoyance (knowing what is not perceptible to the senses), telepathy (mind reading), psychokinesis (moving a physical object by powers of the mind), and precognition (predicting the future).[60] Drawing on the domain of the nonempirical and the unconscious, these can contribute enormously, says the New Age, to heightened consciousness and thus to one's enhanced well-being. But because such powers can be used in an ethical way to accomplish good, they can also help encourage a practical consciousness of responsibility for others. Combined with a sense of a unified humanity, such dispositions foster spiritualist temperaments and activities.

At work in spiritualism is supposed correspondence with those who have passed from this present earthly mode of existence, namely those who have died, and who seem to desire communication with the living. Contact with the dead may take the form of seances or of channeling. In the first instance a mood is set amid a group of people, usually in the dark, where the voice of the departed person or spirit is heard or the person's presence is manifested in some other tangible or visible way. In channeling the departed person or spirit speaks through the voice, mannerisms, or writings of a medium who claims to be in tune with the other world.[61] Several profound and respectable written works have been produced by authors claiming inspiration in this kind of setting.[62] Through procedures like these the New Age professes to find the truth of the ages because of contact with those whose wisdom is expanded by views from the other side of death.

11. We need to trust the divine.

All of the above principles are ordered toward moving the self beyond the ego so that harmony and bliss may become universal indicators of holistic development. All are ordered to provoking mistrust for the distracting and transitory and, at the same time, to eliciting trust for that noble whole of which all is a part and toward which all is developing. Such trust is nurtured through an ennobling union with the one reality of which all appears to be a part. The New Age, identifying this one with what is commonly called the divine,[63] is thus viewed by certain scholars as a multifaceted nontraditional counterforce to modern secularism.[64] This one is the sacred that is characteristic of all reality, of nature, of humanity, and of the very universe.[65]

Union with the one becomes apparent as radical or deep-felt reliance on the divine as such and above all else.[66] Thus, being part of the divine is not just a state in which to be or exist but also a way of choosing, being sure, and becoming whole. To trust the divine that is one with the self is to tap one's greatest potentials and one's highest powers of creativity.[67] It means both willingness to be flexible and success in giving up the ego in favor of a holistically developing self.[68] It means surrendering to what is beyond one's ego-control.[69]

Eleven Principles of the
New Age Movement
and Their Relationship
to Consciousness

1. Everything is divine, including human consciousness.

2. Truth is constituted from within.

3. Growth in consciousness or overcoming faulty consciousness is the key to blissful living and the immediate goal of all enlightened persons.

4. Death leads to reincarnation.

5. There are numerous valid paths to divinity.

6. The attainment of bliss involves concern for the good of all.

7. Health means wholeness and unity of body, mind, and spirit.

8. The unity of all requires closeness to and respect for nature.

9. We need to trust intuition, imagination, and feeling.

10. We need to trust paranormal phenomena.

11. We need to trust the divine.

Notes

1. Doug Boyd, *Mysteries, Magicians, and Medicine People: Tales of a Wanderer* (New York: Paragon House, 1989); John Clancy et al., *A New Age Guide for the Thoroughly Confused and Absolutely Certain* (Eastsound, WA: Sweet Forever, 1988); Alice Dowd, "The 'New Age' for Libraries," *Library Journal* 114 (July 1989), 44–50; Alice Dowd, "What's New in the New Age," *Library Journal* 116 (March 15, 1991), 58–61; *The Fireside Treasury of Light*, ed. Mary Olsen Kelly (New York: Simon & Schuster, 1990); J. Gordon Melton et al., *New Age Encyclopedia* (Detroit: Gale Research, 1990); *The New Age Dictionary: A Guide to Planetary Consciousness*, ed. Alex Jack (Tokyo: Japan Publications, 1990); Christof Schorsch, "Utopie und Mythos der Neuen Zeit: zur Promblemtik des 'New Age'," *Theologische Rundshau* 5 (1989), 315–30.

2. C.G. Jung, *Memories, Dreams, Reflections*, trans. Richard and Clara Winston (New York: Vintage, 1989), 189, 347–48.

3. Pierre Teilhard de Chardin, *The Future of Man*, trans. Norman Denny (New York: Harper, 1964), 95–96, 173–74.

4. Joseph Chilton Pearce, *The Crack in the Cosmic Egg* (New York: Julian, 1971), 97, 109.

5. W. Brugh Joy, "A Heretic in a New Age Community," in *Meeting the Shadow: The Hidden Power of the Dark Side of Human Nature*, eds. Jeremiah Abrams and Connie Zweig (Los Angeles: Tarcher, 1991), 151.

6. J. Gordon Melton, "A Brief History of the New Age Movement," in *New Age Almanac*, 6.

7. William Warch, *New Thought*, 8.

8. Michael Talbot, *Beyond the Quantum* (New York: Macmillan, 1986), 41–46.

9. David Bohm and F. David Peat, *Science, Order, and Creativity* (New York: Bantam, 1987), 172–86.

10. Warch, *New Thought*, 15–16.

11. *A Course in Miracles* (Tiburon, CA: Foundation for Inner Peace, 1975), 68–69.

12. Ken Wilber, *No Boundary: Eastern and Western Approaches to Personal Growth* (Boston: Shambhala, 1979), 143–45.

13. Ken Wilber, "Two Modes of Knowing" in *Beyond Ego: Transpersonal Dimensions in Psychology*, eds. Roger N Walsh and Frances Vaughn (Los Angeles: Tarcher, 1980), 236.

14. Gregory Bateson and Mary Catherine Bateson, *Angels Fear: Towards an Epistemology of the Sacred* (New York: Macmillan, 1987), 183–200.

15. Wilber, *No Boundary*, 25–29.

16. Talbot, *Beyond the Quantum*, 49–50.

17. Marilyn Ferguson, "Karl Pribam's Changing Reality" in *The Holographic Paradigm and Other Paradoxes: Exploring the Leading Edge of Science*, ed. Ken Wilber (Boston: Shambhala, 1982), 15–26.

18. Marilyn Ferguson, *The Aquarian Conspiracy: Personal and Social Transformation in the 1980s* (Los Angeles: Tarcher, 1980), 378.

19. *Course in Miracles*, 21–22, 27, 44.

20. Warch, *New Thought*, 27.

21. Fritjof Capra, *The Tao of Physics* (New York: Bantam, 1977), 266.

22. *Course in Miracles*, 57.

23. *Course in Miracles*, 11, 15, 116.

24. *Course in Miracles*, 115–17; Wilber, *No Boundary*, 7–10, 52–55.

25. Frances Vaughan, *The Inward Arc: Healing and Wholeness in Psychotherapy and Spirituality* (Boston: Shambhala, 1986), 66–67.

26. Gloria D. Karpinski, *Where Two Worlds Touch* (New York: Ballantine, 1990), 89–95.

27. *Course in Miracles*, 75; Gary Zukav, *The Seat of the Soul* (New York: Simon & Schuster, 1989), 35–37.

28. Ram Dass, *Grist for the Mill* (New York: Bantam, 1981), 66–68, 90.

29. David Spangler, *Emergence: The Rebirth of the Sacred* (New York: Simon & Schuster, 1989), 41.

30. Wilber, *No Boundary*, 3.

31. Fritjof Capra, *Uncommon Wisdom: Conversations with Remarkable People* (New York: Simon & Schuster, 1988), 49–53.

32. Ferguson, *Aquarian Conspiracy*, 402–3.

33. Jane Roberts, *The Individual and the Nature of Mass Events* (New York: Prentice Hall, 1981), 7.

34. David Spangler, *Revelation: The Birth of a New Age* (San Francisco: Rainbow Bridge, 1976), 55–62, 87–93.

35. J. A. English–Lueck, *Health in the New Age: A Study in California Holistic Practices* (Albuquerque: University of New Mexico, 1990), 19–20.

36. Vaughan, *Inward Arc*, 10–23.

37. Ferguson, *Aquarian Conspiracy*, 248–64.

38. Capra, *Uncommon Wisdom*, 151.

39. Alberto Villoldo and Stanley Krippner, *Healing States* (New York: Simon & Schuster, 1986).

40. Bernie S. Siegel, *Peace, Love and Healing: Bodymind Communication and the Path to Self-Healing: An Exploration* (New York: Harper, 1989), 18–19, 124.

41. Charlene Spretnak, *States of Grace: The Recovery of Meaning in the Postmodern Age* (San Francisco: Harper, 1991), 20.

42. James Lovelock, *The Ages of Gaia: A Biography of Our Living Earth* (New York: Norton, 1988), 16–19.

43. Gregory Bateson, *Mind and Nature, a Necessary Unity* (New York: Dutton, 1979), 17–18.

44. Zukav, *Seat of the Soul*, 53–57.

45. Spangler, *Emergence*, 49.

46. Roberts, *Individual and Mass Events*, 48.

47. Charlene Spretnak, *The Spiritual Dimension of Green Politics* (Santa Fe, NM: Bear, 1986), 23, 54–55.

48. Capra, *Uncommon Wisdom*, 109.

49. Charlene Spretnak and Fritjof Capra, *Green Politics* (Santa Fe, NM: Bear, 1986), 29–56.

50. John D. Rea, *Healing and Quartz Crystals: A Journey with Our Souls* (Boulder, CO: Two Trees, 1986), *xxiii*, 3–6, 47–51.

51. Vaughan, *Inward Arc*, 39–49.

52. Bateson, *Mind and Nature*, 32–38.

53. Capra, *Uncommon Wisdom*, 67–70.

54. Ferguson, *Aquarian Conspiracy*, 77–79.

55. Vaughan, *Inward Arc*, 155–65.

56. Capra, *Tao of Physics*, 27–28, 60, 122–23, 188, 228.

57. Ferguson, *Aquarian Conspiracy*, 148–50; Capra, *Tao of Physics*, 292.

58. Wilber, *No Boundary*, 33–43; Capra, *Tao of Physics*, 197.

59. Talbot, *Beyond the Quantum*, 53–54.

60. Ferguson, *Aquarian Conspiracy*, 174–76.

61. Karpinski, *Two Worlds*, 177–79.

62. Roger N. Walsh, *The Spirit of Shamanism* (Los Angeles: Tarcher, 1990), 123–30.

63. Clancy, *New Age Guide*, 103–7.

64. Detlef Pollach, "Vom Tischrücken zur Psychodynamik: Formen ausserkirchlicher Religiosität in Deutschland," *Schweizerische Zeitschrift für Soziologie/Revue Suisse de sociologie* 16, no.1 (November 1990), 107–34.

65. Fox, *Cosmic Christ*, 8.
66. Zukav, *Seat of the Soul*, 240–46.
67. Ken Carey, *Return of the Bird Tribes* (New York: Uni-Sun, 1988), 151-52.
68. Jeremy Tarcher, "New Age as Perennial Philosophy: What the Media Missed," *New Realities* (May–June 1988), 27.
69. Karpinski, *Two Worlds*, 32.

CHAPTER 3

Emergence and Hope– Biblical Beginnings

Genesis 1–4, 6, 9, 11–12, 15, 22, 28, 30–32, 40, 44

MAKING THE COMPARISONS

Keeping in mind the eleven principles of the New Age as they were discussed in the last chapter, I have interpreted selected biblical texts in order to consider their relationship to New Age teaching and practice. My examination of the scriptural material focuses on Genesis, Wisdom literature and Psalms, Luke's gospel, and the Pauline literature. The treatment thus includes a limited selection of readings from the Bible's many books. The comparisons and contrasts that emerge, however, seem to me to be typical of what can be said of the Bible as a whole because of its mosaiclike coherence. Since the most characteristic perspectives, concepts, and themes of the Bible harmonize, the concerns of the selected texts by and large overlap or accord with the interests of the Bible's other chapters and books. Clearly, various entries into the world of biblical religion are possible. The texts I have chosen appear in light of this book's goals to be particularly helpful or cogent.

As examination and comparison of the texts occur, it will be important to remember that the principles of the New Age movement are being offered only as points of reference. They are not criteria or standards for determining definitively the meaning of the biblical texts. Such criteria might exist in the mind and heart of an individual whose faith is rooted in biblical teaching. They also might exist in an individual community of faith, like a given denomination or church, so that members of such a community sense a general solidarity in their beliefs. For example, the doctrines of a particular church may be regarded as indispensable for understanding what the Bible says about the relationship of God to creation or of Christ to the believer. The principles of the New Age are not proposed as having such authority. Rather, they are assumed to represent interests that guide examination and interpretation, as interest in liberation guides many biblical interpretations today without claiming to provide the last word on biblical understanding. In line with the processes of historical and reader response criticism as discussed in the first chapter of this book, the principles of the New Age movement provide tentative vantage points from which to assess the Bible's religious message. They are a place from which to begin.

MARRING THE ORIGINAL DESIGN

The creation account of Genesis has been called by some scholars a cosmological myth, an etiological myth, or a primeval history. Such terminology refers to the power of the story to communicate a perspective on the ultimate origin of the universe and to depict the basic structure of all things. Having to do with the transcendent or divine, myths appear to stand in their own right as forms of communication equal to science, or any other form of scholarship, that deals with given realities from its own perspectives.[1] In other words, myths speak in their own figurative or symbolic language about truths of life or creation; they are a kind of poetry that expresses deep and compelling meanings as persuasively as a science can communicate its own kind of findings according to its particular methods and formulas.

Mythological stories, often overtly religious in nature, can communicate their visions whether they are factual or not, even as parables teach moral or religious lessons whether they are based on historical incidents or not. The Genesis story, having in endless debates been called both fact and fiction, nevertheless communicates a profound religious perspective on reality, namely a teaching that God is the ultimate originator and orderer of a creation meant by the divine plan to be wholly good but which has been defiled by evil swaying human choice and so leading to human maliciousness. After acts that counter God's commands, man and woman's formerly innocent presence becomes a possible source of shame:

> *they knew that they were naked (3:7).*

In a state of perfect obedience to God, they had enjoyed a blessed intimacy with the divine. Moreover, their relationship with one another had been in no way subject to abuses of manipulation, passion, or self-deprecation. Distance from God, however, brought with it immanent threats of increased distance from harmonious relationships with themselves, one another, and their environments. Woman's specific plight is

> *'in pain . . . (to) bring forth children' (3:16).*

And because the earth is now full of "thorns and thistles" (3:18), the man must toil and sweat (3:17–19). The ultimate disruption of God's original design is death:

> *'For you are dust,*
> *and to dust you shall return' (3:19b).*

A history of disobedience, begun by the man and the woman in the garden, disturbs the original order and culminates in the destruction of the earth by flood. This history parallels the infidelity of God's chosen people, the nation Israel, in its disobedience from Moses on in face of the Law, in face of the divine stipulations by which this people was to live. For Israel suffered from a recurrent pride, a sense of self-righteousness that amounted, for those who knew better, to a kind of idolatry. Israel's sins, often manifested as outright worship of other gods or as neglect of persons in need, culminated in the devastation of Jerusalem and the remaining southern kingdom some seven hundred years after Moses.

GOD'S MERCY

At every stage of the primeval history in Genesis however, as at every stage of Israel's later failings, God's compassion shows forth and instills hope for the future. The God of mercy — the Lord of Israel who would rescue it from slavery in Egypt and from captivity in Babylon, the Lord God who would remain faithful to the chosen people — allows humans superiority over the wily serpent who through temptation has introduced humans to prideful disobedience. God tells the serpent:

> *'I will put enmity between you and the woman,*
> *and between your offspring and hers;*
> *he will strike your head,*
> *and you will strike his heel' (3:15).*

In the context of the entire Bible's witness to God's methods, and by longstanding interpretation in Christianity, these words have been seen as a testimony to God's desire to help a weakened humanity win the struggle against evil. The devious forces that disrupt the harmony between humanity and God must ultimately succumb to a debilitating blow. By the power of God, evil is to be overcome and human maliciousness to be rendered powerless.

But God's mercy does not stop here. Death had been established as the penalty for self-righteousness, for eating from the tree of the knowledge of good and evil (2:16-17). God suspends that penalty and replaces it with expulsion from the garden and with unrelenting labor:

> *The LORD God sent him forth from the garden of Eden, to till the*
> *ground from which he was taken (3:23).*

Later, even the murderous Cain, condemned to wander in restlessness, is by God's own words protected from untimely annihilation:

> *'Whoever kills Cain will suffer a sevenfold vengeance.' And the LORD*
> *put a mark on Cain, so that no one who came upon him would kill*
> *him (4:15).*

Among the descendants of the original couple are Noah and his children. Amid rampant evil, God promises to protect this innocent family from imminent destruction and to reserve for it a special gift:

> *Noah was a righteous man, blameless in his generation. 'I will establish my covenant with you; and you shall come into the ark, you, your sons, your wife, and your sons' wives with you' (6:9, 18).*

After the destructive flood God vows never to doom the earth in such a manner again:

> *'I will never again curse the ground because of humankind, for the inclination of the human heart is evil from youth; nor will I ever again destroy every living creature as I have done' (8:21).*

In fact, from the multiplicity of generations and nations that sprang from Noah's family, God prepares the way for the chosen people.

> *Terah took his son Abram and his grandson Lot son of Haran, and his daughter-in-law Sarai, his son Abram's wife, and they went out together from Ur of the Chaldeans to go into the land of Canaan (11:31).*

TRUST, LIKENESS, AND RENEWAL

Looking to these chapters of Genesis for a comparison with the New Age, we can find clear agreement of the biblical perspective with the notion that the divine is master of our destinies and is eminently trustworthy. Not to trust or obey is to merit degradation or ruin. Such disobedience — going contrary to what is godly — is really a matter of self-alienation or harm to self since by nature humans are like the divine. They have a godly stamp. Having molded them in the divine image, God created them "male and female" (1:27).

The anthropology here — the way humans are understood to be constituted — does not proclaim the absolute divinity of humans but does depict a profound intimacy that allows for parallelism or cooperation in divine and human activity, especially with regard to the production of human life and to dominion over nature. In such areas God and humans should be partners.

> *God blessed them, and God said to them, 'Be fruitful and multiply, and fill the earth and subdue it; and have dominion over the fish of the sea and over the birds of the air and over every living thing that moves upon the earth' (1:28).*

Human dominion over the earth should parallel and partake in God's dominion over the universe.[2] Dominion of this kind is not a license for abuse and irresponsibility but is an awesome charge that requires care and responsible decisions.[3] The defiling of creation, which human self-alienating disobedience provokes, reveals a sense of what the New Age might call a holistic view of humanity and nature, a perspective in which the elements of creation are seen to relate to one another in their well-being. Since they are meant to live in harmony with nature, humans merely hurt themselves when they eat the forbidden fruit, when they try to be masters of things beyond their dominion, or when they violate the limits set on their use of nature and its products.

In the perspective of this narrative the ultimate penalty is a death into the darkness of the earth, into the dust to which humans must return. Yet the banishment from the original garden in which all was very good shows that the Bible already knows that after acts that merit death, a lenient God can allow another chance. This second opportunity is not the same as the multiple life-opportunities that the New Age knows as reincarnation, but the processes parallel in that God or the divine establishes time for renewal. In the biblical view the renewal must essentially take place within one lifetime. With reincarnation the renewal may take place over many lifetimes. One can imagine advantages and disadvantages in each view. Both however reflect that the immediate result of human failure is hardly immediate and definitive vindictiveness or punishment.

THE QUESTION OF OTHER RELIGIONS

If *some* overlap between the Bible and the New Age is apparent regarding divine mercy and human renewal, *little* seems to be visible with respect to the nature of true religion. For quite unlike the

New Age, these chapters take an exclusionist view regarding other religions. In other words, other religions are regarded as somehow lacking. The gods and institutions of other religions, particularly those associated with sexual activity, are portrayed as nothing.

This doctrine appears to be implicit first of all in establishing the creaturely status of the heavenly bodies:

> *God made the two great lights – the greater light to rule the day and the lesser light to rule the night – and the stars (1:16).*

Other religions regarded these celestial bodies as deities. The narrative here makes clear that they are products of the one God's creative activity.[4] Secondly, fertility is said to rest in nature as designed by God:

> *The earth brought forth vegetation: plants yielding seed of every kind, and trees of every kind bearing fruit with the seed in it. And God saw that it was good (1:12).*

To other creatures God says,

> *'Be fruitful and multiply and fill the waters in the seas, and let birds multiply on the earth' (1:22).*

A similar directive is given to the man and woman. Fertility thus lies in divinely fashioned biological or gender characteristics rather than in the powers of deities. Other religions reverenced such deities through fertility cults, forms of worship often involving sexual activity. The narrative here displays no faith in them. Israel's God is thus presented as the single object of religious faith; other religions, at least by implication, are given diminished status.

Yet Genesis is not entirely closed to the goodness of human beings who do not recognize the God of Israel. The covenant that God makes with Noah and for which God gives the rainbow as a sign is made for the whole earth and all its people:

> *This is the sign of the covenant that I make between me and you and every living creature that is with you, for all future generations: I have set my bow in the clouds, and it shall be a sign of the covenant between me and the earth' (9:12-13).*

This is not like New Age pluralism regarding religions — not a tolerance for all religions as equally valid — but a recognition that what the chosen people professed as the divine has a benevolent relationship with all peoples no matter what their religious persuasions. Genesis thus sees its deity as a God of universal love and compassion.

ADMIRABLE FAITH

If in primeval history Israel found parallels to its own struggles and hopes under the covenant, it could likewise do so with regard to its immediate ancestors, the patriarchs, who bridged the gap from Noah to Moses. Abraham, Isaac, Jacob, and the latter's twelve sons (including Joseph) are for much historical criticism not simply factual ancestors but also or primarily symbols of Israel's later history. Many readers are unsatisfied with such a view and feel that the patriarchs are historical personalities. Whatever the case, of prime importance in their stories are the ancestors' exemplary actions that are carried out under the direction of God.

As the father of the Hebrew people, Abram (later Abraham) sets a good example by being willing to leave a situation of security and enter a new territory:

> The LORD said to Abram, 'Go from your country and your kindred and your father's house to the land that I will show you' (12:1).

For he has a special destiny:

> 'In you all the families of the earth shall be blessed' (12:3b).

Here he exemplifies the elected Israel's destiny on behalf of all nations. Through this chosen people, God and the religion by which the divine is known will be available throughout the world.

What was indispensable however was Abram's great virtue, which was of a special sort:

> He believed the LORD; and the LORD reckoned it to him as righteousness (15:6).

He and his wife Sarah were advanced in age and would have otherwise had no hope for children. But through faith, the seemingly
impossible is accepted as possible, and the totally unreal becomes
reality.

Bridging the covenants of Noah and Sinai, God makes a
covenant with Abram. The setting for this was the split carcasses of
a heifer, goat, and ram through which a burning brazier and blaz-
ing torch passed while Abram slumbered or — as the Hebrew text
also suggests — fell into a trance.

> *As the sun was going down, a deep sleep fell upon Abram, and a deep
> and terrifying darkness descended upon him (15:12).*

He endured the experience however and sealed the covenant
offered by God. Such great faith is paralleled by the magnificence
of his obedience when he is asked to sacrifice his son Isaac. But
God's messenger (an angel) intervenes in time.

> *'Do not lay your hand on the boy or do anything to him; for now I
> know that you fear God, since you have not withheld your son, your
> only son, from me' (22:12).*

ADMIRABLE SELF-ASSURANCE

In Genesis 28, Abraham's son Isaac sends his own son Jacob to the
latter's uncle Laban in order to find a wife. Isaac's prayer is that the
blessing on Abraham may be kept alive through Jacob.

> *'May he (God) give to you the blessing of Abraham, to you and to your
> offspring with you, so that you may take possession of the land where
> you now live as an alien — land that God gave to Abraham' (28:4).*

Along the way Jacob rests at Bethel, a holy place. In a dream his
connection to heaven via a stairway or ladder is revealed. Here
God reiterates the promise made to Abraham and Isaac.

> *'I am the LORD, the God of Abraham your father and the God of Isaac;
> the land on which you lie I will give to you and to your offspring'
> (28:13).*

Upon awaking, Jacob displays great trust in the dream and inter-prets it with reference to the holiness of the place.

> 'Surely the LORD is in this place – and I did not know it!' And he was afraid, and said, 'How awesome is this place! This is none other than the house of God, and this is the gate of heaven' (28:16-17).

In Laban's country Jacob increases and multiplies, begetting children through his wives and their servant-girls (30:1-24) in accord with accepted practice of the time. The twelve boys would become the heads of the twelve tribes of Israel. His uncle knows very well how enriching Jacob's presence has been but is appar-ently reluctant to give Jacob his full recompense:

> 'I have learned by divination that the LORD has blessed me because of you' (30:27b).

Later

> God came to Laban the Aramaean in a dream by night, and said to him, 'Take heed that you say not a word to Jacob, either good or bad' (31:24).

But in order to secure generous compensation for his accomplish-ments, Jacob entices Laban to agree to only uncommonly colored goats and sheep as pay. Laban welcomes this apparent opportunity to get off easily. Then Jacob ingeniously uses striped rods to breed new stocks.

> The flocks bred in front of the rods, and so the flocks produced young that were striped, speckled, and spotted. Jacob separated the lambs, and set the faces of the flocks toward the striped and the completely black animals in the flock of Laban; and he put his own droves apart, and did not put them with Laban's flock (30:39-40).

Eventually Jacob decides to return to his homeland, not how-ever before he reminds the Lord of the promise to protect him and bless him.

> *You have said, 'I will surely do you good, and make your offspring as the sand of the sea, which cannot be counted because of their number'* (32:12).

His concern in the matter is great, for he fears resistance from his brother Esau. The reminder confirms as well the boldness with which Jacob relates to God. At the stream of Jabbok, Jacob struggles with an agent of the Lord and with typical persistence beats the opponent. Thus he is given the new identity and named "Israel."

> *Then the man said, 'You shall no longer be called Jacob, but Israel, for you have striven with God and with humans, and have prevailed'* (32:28).

Jacob then realizes that he had "seen God face to face" (32:30). He, or Israel, is thus the one who contends with God and wins.

RESPECT FOR DREAMS

The way is prepared for the Exodus when Joseph, one of Jacob's sons, finds his way into Egypt. Genesis 37 tells us that he was the most loved of the sons. The animosity of the brothers toward him, as well as Israel's (Jacob's) discomfort with his intimations at ascendancy or superiority over them, was fired by their respect for the revelatory power of his dreams.

> *'Are you indeed to reign over us? Are you indeed to have dominion over us?' So they hated him even more because of his dreams and his words. But when he told it to his father and to his brothers, his father rebuked him, and said to him, 'What kind of dream is this that you have had? Shall we indeed come, I and your mother and your brothers, and bow to the ground before you?'* (37:8, 10)

Joseph shares their appreciation of dreams as well as the belief that interpreting them is a divinely inspired talent.

> *They said to him, 'We have had dreams, and there is no one to inter-*
> *pret them.' And Joseph said to them, 'Do not interpretations belong to*
> *God? Please tell them to me' (40:8).*

Once he is sold into slavery in Egypt, this talent allows Joseph eventually to gain stature in Pharaoh's eyes. Thus Joseph could work toward assuming the status that would allow him to receive his father and brothers into Egypt when they migrated from Canaan, the land promised to Abraham and his descendants.

FAITH AND UNIVERSALISM

We do not need to look very hard in these latter chapters of Genesis to find elements that correspond with New Age interests. Clearly, Abraham is a model of trust, both in moving into the strange and foreign land of Canaan, in braving the terror of entering the covenant with God, and in being willing to sacrifice his son without question. His obedient faith that issues in such trust makes him the model of the dispositions expected of the man and the woman in the creation story that preceded the saga of Abraham and his family. He thus models the disposition that, according to Israel's faith, God requests of Abraham's children, his immediate ones and those in the long line after him. The whole Bible shows how the loyal descendants and successors of Abraham, whether Jewish or otherwise, are enlivened by such faith and rewarded for it. In the matter of trusting the divine, the Bible and the New Age already appear to have much in common.

God's promise to make Abraham the father of many nations continues the universalist thrust of the rainbow covenant. I proposed above that this covenant suggests divine interest in all peoples in a way that parallels, though quite limitedly, New Age pluralism respecting the variety of religions in the world. The same kind of parallel can be seen in the covenant with Abraham. It shows God's readiness to bless all humanity, a generosity that the New Age finds reflected in all true religions' ability to lead toward divinity. What limits the parallel however is the Bible's suggestion here and later that universal oneness with God will come through a common religious practice.

IMAGINATION, THE UNCONSCIOUS, AND HIGHER CONSCIOUSNESS

But Genesis presents Abraham as the model of true religion. He interacts familiarly with the divine. At one point his covenant with God is depicted as an occurrence in sleep or a trance. Like sleep, a trance is an altered state of consciousness in which, by modern psychological perspectives, the unconscious appears to be highly activated. In the New Age view such states are frequently regarded as important for sensing or influencing other dimensions of reality. The highly charged symbols of the torch and smoking oven reveal the biblical author's sensitivity to the power of appealing to the imagination. From its earliest books the Bible, like the New Age, demonstrates interest in appealing to what is called today the "right brain." Such interest, in modern perspectives, utilizes images that appeal to the unconscious in a beneficial way. Abraham thus interacts with God through vibrant images and cooperates in setting the precedent for the future interaction of God and the people of Israel.

When God seemed to be asking for the sacrifice of Isaac, Abraham again demonstrated an extraordinary capacity to interact directly with God. Biblical interpreters of differing convictions can argue how Abraham heard the message of the angel. An inner awareness, an audible voice, a vision, and more are possibilities. But that he interacted with God in a paranormal way is spoken of routinely. Such experience does not fit every modern scientific view of reality. The New Age however is becoming increasingly at home with experiences of this kind and is quite inclined to find that as so described they accord with its own expectations regarding contact with the world of the nonempirical or divine.

It is reasonable or apparently even necessary to assume that the author or authors of Genesis *intended* to write history and not merely a series of purely figurative stories. The tone and contours of the book appear to be such that this assumption is defensible even if by certain modern standards some or parts of the stories cannot be accepted as literally historical.[5] Standards however change. And the criteria of the New Age are affecting what many today accept as possible or realistic and thus acceptable as historical in the literal sense.

That interaction with God can be quite concrete is suggested by Jacob's wrestling with the angel at Jabbok. Whether the story is historical or not, it suggests that the inspired writer hardly feels that such a scenario is beyond the credence of the readers or listeners. Nor does it appear to be problematic for the biblical writers to assume that God reveals important matters in dreams, as the occurrence of dreams in the Jacob and Joseph stories indicate. Sometimes their meanings are self-evident; sometimes they need to be interpreted. This is consonant with the New Age approach to the imagination as a vehicle to the unconscious. Here dreams can play an important role, and a respectable interpretation of them can be part of determining what course one is on in life or what course one should take.

Accepting the literalness of Jacob's unusual skills in breeding the animals of desired color is undoubtedly hard for many readers or listeners today. Again, however, the biblical writer appears to be assuming that it is not asking too much to expect one to imagine that, with divine concurrence, one can ingeniously influence a course of events in calculative and extraordinary ways.[6] Such ways might also be called paranormal. It may be going too far to regard Jacob's methodology as an example of psychokinesis or the influencing of physical happenings through powers of the mind. For according to the story, the presence of striped rods and dark cattle, not Jacob's intentions alone, were part of achieving the desired end.

Yet Jacob did intend things to go as they did, and there is no visible influence of the stripes and colors on the markings of the new kids and calves. Something similar can be said of the blessings on Laban and the divination that revealed them to him as such. Divination, a paranormal practice respected by many of the New Age, is a technique of attaining, in some extraordinary way, knowledge of something not immediately apparent. The knowledge can be of something present but hidden or of something not present but coming. The diviner is not visibly influenced by whatever is known. The contact between them cannot be seen. Genesis 44:4–5 suggests — and without judgment[7] — that Jacob's son Joseph practiced divination by reading the contents of a goblet. The author of the text would likely have known that the custom, here practiced by a Hebrew patriarch, was common among ancient Egyptians.[8] Equally well established in the ancient Near East was dream interpretation regarded as operative under divine influence.[9] So, Joseph's specialization in such interpretation would have been highly valued.

Moreover, in ancient Israel the Urim and Thummim were small objects carried in the high priest's breast piece (Ex 28:30) and used, especially in Israel's earlier history, for divining the Lord's will (1 Sm 28:6). Such communication was regarded as inerrant.[10] The priestly custom of associating the breast piece with power to speak for God was adapted from the religious practice of Israel's neighbors, the Canaanites.[11] In several places (e.g., Jos 18:10) Hebrew Scripture mentions divination that takes place by the casting of lots.[12] As Proverbs 16:33 puts it:

> When the lot is cast into the lap, its decision depends entirely on the LORD.

In modern times Carl Jung has spoken of synchronicity, when events relate meaningfully to one another but not because one has directly caused the other. A higher energy goes to work, a spiritual energy, says the New Age, that connects consciousness and the awaited event.[13] If the rods and adult cattle did not cause the colors of the baby animals, their colors occur as meaningfully related to what Jacob had in mind. If the blessings on Laban did not cause the diviner to know of them, their existence is meaningfully related to the diviner's awareness. What happened, then, in both the case of the animals and the case of the divination was not merely coincidental. A larger dimension of the situation needs to be considered. In this case, according to Genesis, the larger dimension involves the cooperative presence of God.

The association of mind to matter, events, or relationships is further considered when the biblical author depicts Jacob's contention with God or God's agent as a kind of victory. Wrestling through the night, the two appear to be evenly matched.[14] Overall the extraordinary amount of self-will in Jacob's activities would seem to be teaching that response to the divine is not always a matter of pure passivity. The story, teaching how an authentic and empowering relationship with God can involve strife and wrestling,[15] resembles other ancient tales in which a person's struggle with deities results in extracting godly powers and secrets from them.[16]

The admirable patriarch, Jacob, has been consistently portrayed in Genesis as assertive and ingenious. For the New Age too, human energy and personal responsibility are of prime importance to growth in consciousness and in helpfulness on behalf of others and the world. But the higher consciousness and determined will, which not only know but also determine outcomes in one's world, are thought to operate with true profit only when accorded with the unifying one, only when linked with trust in the divine and with obedience to the divine will.[17] Likewise Jacob's ascendancy over God was not so much superiority over God but was more a display of strength required to be a champion of God's will. God is not overcome, teaches Genesis, only *overtaken*.

Notes

1. John L. McKenzie, *A Theology of the Old Testament* (Garden City, NY: Doubleday, 1974), 181.

2. Robert P. Meye, "Invitation to Wonder: Toward a Theology of Nature" in *Tending the Garden*, 46–48; William Dyrness, "Stewardship of the Earth in the Old Testament" in *Tending the Garden*, 53, 64.

3. Bruce Vawter, *On Genesis: A New Reading* (Garden City, NY: Doubleday, 1977), 59–60.

4. Vawter, *On Genesis*, 48.

5. Vawter, *On Genesis*, 30–33.

6. Claus Westermann, *Genesis 12–36: A Commentary*, trans. John J. Scullion (Minneapolis: Augsburg, 1985), 483–84.

7. Vawter, *On Genesis*, 430.

8. Claus Westermann, *Genesis 37–50: A Commentary*, trans. John J. Scullion (Minneapolis: Augsburg, 1986), 132.

9. W. Lee Humphreys, *Joseph and His Family: A Literary Study* (Columbia, SC: University of South Carolina, 1988), 74, 110, 121–22, 166–69.

10. William McKane, *Proverbs: A New Approach* (Philadelphia: Westminster, 1970), 499.

11. Gerhard von Rad, *Old Testament Theology* (New York: Harper, 1962), 1:24.

12. Walter Eichrodt, *Theology of the Old Testament*, trans J. A. Baker (Philadelphia: Westminster, 1961), 1:113–14.

13. Karpinski, *Two Worlds*, 163–68.

14. Walter Brueggemann, *Genesis* (Atlanta: John Knox, 1982), 267.

15. Vawter, *On Genesis*, 351.

16. Gerhard von Rad, *Genesis: A Commentary* (Philadelphia: Westminster, 1972), 321.

17. Spangler, *Revelation*, 131–32.

CHAPTER 4

Practical Holiness – Israel's Wisdom and Prayer

Proverbs 6, 15–16, 20, 26; Psalms 1, 8, 25, 41, 73, 132, 148, 150

BIBLICAL WISDOM

In Genesis there is a strong interest in origins or ancestral history. With the Psalms and Wisdom literature the focus is different, though concerns for creation and ancestors are not entirely absent. The Psalms show a strong interest in piety and worship. The Wisdom writings, sometimes referred to as the sapiential works, show interest in edifying everyday conduct and, more philosophically, in life's "big" questions. These are associated with such weighty matters as justice, evil, and death. Some of the psalms treat themes like these and show influences of Israel's sapiential traditions.

The philosophical discussions of the Wisdom literature have parallels among ancient peoples such as the Canaanites and Egyptians. The sages or wise ones of Israel probably borrowed from such people as these and adapted the Gentile wisdom to Israel's traditional faith. This was in keeping with the general custom of Israel — as numerous examples throughout the Bible attest — to adapt to its own religion the beliefs and practices of other peoples. Such adaptation may provide a lesson for those who see resemblances though perhaps not identicalness between biblical and New Age teachings. Either group can learn from the other and reshape the other's teachings by standards deemed appropriate.

71

PROVERBS: DILIGENCE IN THE RIGHT THINGS

The Bible's sapiential traditions teach that the greatest wisdom is a gift from God; it comes with knowing and doing God's will. On a smaller but still important scale, wisdom is awareness that comes through familiarity with practical virtues. The Book of Proverbs contains a large collection of sayings that constitute a treasury of guidelines for daily living. Below the surface is a firm moral code that orients the author's designs to persuade the reader into following a reputable lifestyle. There appears to be no distinction between secular and religious life since from the author's perspective all wise conduct is essentially part of a life of faith.[1] One of the most emphasized virtues is diligence:

> Go to the ant, you lazybones;
>> consider its ways, and be wise (6:6).
> The lazy person does not plow in season;
>> harvest comes, and there is nothing to be found (20:4).
> As a door turns on its hinges,
>> so does a lazy person in bed (26:14).
> The lazy person buries a hand in the dish,
>> and is too tired to bring it back to the mouth (26:15).

But industriousness is not to revel in itself. The productive person is one whose creations arise out of trust in the Lord:

> Commit your work to the LORD,
>> and your plans will be established (16:3).

THE WAYS OF THE WISE

The happy combination of personal action and reliance on God is aided by numerous virtues such as justice, patience, sobriety, calmness, and advice-seeking:

> Better is a little with righteousness
>> than large income with injustice (16:8).
> One who is slow to anger is better than the mighty,
>> and one whose temper is controlled than one who
>>> captures a city (16:32).

Wine is a mocker, strong drink a brawler,
*   and whoever is led astray by it is not wise (20:1).*
It is honorable to refrain from strife,
*   but every fool is quick to quarrel (20:3).*
Like a sparrow in its flitting, like a swallow in its flying,
*   an undeserved curse goes nowhere (26:2).*
Plans are established by taking advice;
*   wage war by following wise guidance (20:18).*

Failure to live by such wisdom can lead to dreadful punishments:

Calamity will descend suddenly;
*   in a moment, damage beyond repair (6:15).*
Pride goes before destruction,
*   and a haughty spirit before a fall (16:18).*
Bread gained by deceit is sweet,
*   but afterward the mouth will be full of gravel (20:17).*
A whip for the horse, a bridle for the donkey,
*   and a rod for the back of fools (26:3).*
Whoever digs a pit will fall into it,
*   and a stone will come back on the one who starts it*
*   rolling (26:27).*

On the other hand, recourse to wisdom brings many rewards, including peace, persuasiveness, health, gray hair (called indeed a *reward*), and familial tranquility:

When the ways of people please the Lord,
*   he causes even their enemies to be at peace*
*   with them (16:7).*
The mind of the wise makes their speech judicious,
*   and adds persuasiveness to their lips (16:23).*
Pleasant words are like a honeycomb,
*   sweetness to the soul and health to the body (16:24).*
Gray hair is a crown of glory;
*   it is gained in a righteous life (16:31).*
The righteous walk in integrity—
*   happy are the children who follow them! (20:7)*

THE DOCTRINE OF RETRIBUTION

Like other parts of the Bible, the Wisdom literature teaches that reward for good and punishment for evildoing follow in a kind of natural course. Reward and punishment are ultimately a sign of God's justice, the divine response to human virtue or folly. Commonly known as the doctrine of retribution, this teaching is illustrated in Proverbs with great poignancy. Punishment of course hurts. Therefore from the perspective of the doctrine of retribution, suffering is looked upon as the outcome of negligence, mischief, crime, or sin.

This explanation for suffering is present throughout the Hebrew and Christian Scriptures. It is not however the only explanation. Other views are found in the Wisdom literature as well as in the prophetic books and the gospels. From these perspectives suffering is not always equated with punishment but has other purposes, ones often known only to God. Nor is contentment always equated with virtue, for the wicked often appear to be advantaged. It would be reckless however to gamble on an exception to the doctrine of retribution.

So Proverbs makes it quite clear that anyone not practicing wisdom is a fool.

> The legs of a disabled person hang limp;
> > so does a proverb in the mouth of a fool.
> It is like binding a stone in a sling
> > to give honor to a fool.
> Like a thornbush brandished by the hand of a drunkard
> > is a proverb in the mouth of a fool.
> Like an archer who wounds everybody
> > is one who hires a passing fool or drunkard.
> Like a dog that returns to its vomit
> > is a fool who reverts to his folly (26:7-11).

For wisdom is a great treasure.

> The purposes in the human mind are like deep water,
> > but the intelligent will draw them out (20:5).

> *How much better to get wisdom than gold!*
> *To get understanding is to be chosen rather than silver*
> *(16:16).*

Wisdom comes with practice, but it is not merely a human invention. The greatest teacher is not the sage or wise one, but God, from whom the soundest direction comes, and who is ultimately in charge of all good accomplished:

> *The fear of the LORD is instruction in wisdom,*
> *and humility goes before honor (15:33).*

THE PSALMS: SONGS OF MANY MOODS

The emotionality of the Psalms is hardly surpassed by any other part of biblical literature. The sentiments range from apparent despair to intense joy. The situation is however interpersonal in that these utterances presume communication. They are prayers directed by individuals or communities toward God. The prayers include much more than petition or request, although divine help is frequently something they seek. They are usually candid expressions of feelings shared in a tone that suggests freedom before a God who listens compassionately no matter what is being said. Sometimes they rebuke or scold; sometimes they exult or glorify. We are perhaps not quite as accustomed to berating as well as praising God. The psalmists however do not hesitate to do either. The broad spectrum of their sentiments suggests a spirituality embodied in the wide range of human experiences.

Such breadth can also be seen in the Psalms' many theologies or ways of treating matters related to God. These theologies include the doctrine of retribution and insights of the earlier and later Wisdom literature. The Psalms can be down to earth, or they can sing rapturously of sublime experience and inspiring revelation. In their great diversity they reflect both the practicality and seriousness of wisdom.

TRUE HAPPINESS

Psalm 1 serves as an introduction to the entire collection and is typical of the positive approach that characterizes so many of the psalms. The opening verses assume the validity of the doctrine of retribution and recall that true happiness or blessedness comes with obedience to God.

> *Happy are those*
>> *who do not follow the advice of the wicked,*
> *or take the path that sinners tread,*
>> *or sit in the seat of scoffers;*
> *but their delight is in the law of the LORD (vss 1–2).*

This abstract dictum or adage is then complemented by a beautiful image that gives the statement extra force and feeling. Religiously obedient persons

> *. . . are like trees*
>> *planted by streams of water,*
> *which yield their fruit in its season,*
>> *and their leaves do not wither (vs 3).*

To hear the play of the water or to sense the dignity and generosity of the vigorous tree is to be drawn into the kind of poetry by which the Psalms typically aim to enliven the spirit of one who prays them.

HUMAN POWER IN THE HANDS OF GOD

Psalm 8 continues to emphasize the dignity of human persons and the great power that they enjoy in the hands of God. There is a paradox here in that one individual seems so small compared with the mighty grandeur of the universe. In this context the psalmist says to God:

> *You have set your glory above the heavens (vs 1b).*

Yet by the divine plan every individual participates in that majesty and can draw on it to accomplish wonderful things. As God does, one can act responsibly and creatively in directing life and creation itself toward noble and desirable ends. For, as the prayer to God continues, humans are like angels who have been given

> . . . *dominion over the works of your hands*

since God has decided to subject everything to the men and women who sometime appear to themselves as too limited for such a destiny (vss 2, 5–6). For they have dominion over

> *all sheep and oxen,*
> > *and also the beasts of the field,*
> *the birds of the air, and the fish of the sea,*
> > *whatever passes along the paths of the seas (vss 7-8).*

The imagery suggests that human authority, responsibility, and power extend to all of nature, to all that belongs to life.

THE VALUE OF TRUST

Psalm 25 makes clear that humans do not rightly exercise such dominion with utter autonomy or independence but only under divine guidance. They must thus exhibit trust, a virtue proclaimed recurrently in the psalm.

> *To you, O LORD, I lift up my soul.*
> *O my God, in you I trust;*
> > *do not let me be put to shame;*
> > *do not let my enemies exult over me (vss 1-2).*

One's enemies can be menaces from the outside, like threatening persons or circumstances. More often perhaps, such threateners come from within as perturbing dispositions like envy or resentment. Freedom from their intimidation can be won, but not by one's mere cunning. For, as the wisdom literature teaches, the best knowledge comes from God.

> *Make me to know your ways, O LORD;*
> > *teach me your paths.*

> Lead me in your truth, and teach me,
>> for you are the God of my salvation;
>> for you I wait all day long (vss 4–5).

A requisite of such instruction is humility (vs 9), but so is confidence in God's forgiveness.

> Do not remember the sins of my youth or my transgressions;
>> according to your steadfast love remember me,
>> for your goodness' sake, O LORD!
> For your name's sake, O LORD,
>> pardon my guilt, for it is great.
> Consider my affliction and my trouble,
>> and forgive all my sins.
> May integrity and uprightness preserve me,
>> for I wait for you (vss 7, 11, 18, 21).

HEALTH OF SPIRIT

Psalm 41 reflects a sense of the relationship between sin and illness and between spiritual revival and physical healing. First of all, compassion brings a certain immunity from harm.

> Happy are those who consider the poor;
>> the LORD delivers them in the day of trouble.
> The LORD protects them and keeps them alive;
>> they are called happy in the land.
>> You do not give them up to the will of their enemies (vss 1–2).

Should a compassionate person become afflicted, a sincere and humble confession of sin brings hope in divine help that puts the fiendish attackers to shame.

> As for me, I said, 'O LORD, be gracious to me;
>> heal me, for I have sinned against you.'
> But you, O LORD, be gracious to me,
>> and raise me up, that I may repay them (vss. 4, 10).

This is something that the psalmist knows from experience. Thus the Lord, the granter of every blessing, is to be highly praised.

> *Blessed be the LORD, the God of Israel,*
> > *from everlasting to everlasting. Amen and Amen (vs. 13).*

RETRIBUTION AND BEYOND

Psalm 73, a fine example of a Wisdom psalm, is the kind of prayer that Job would have prayed after his trials. By the time this psalm was composed, suspicions regarding judgment in a future life appear to be strong. In early Hebrew literature there is more uncertainty regarding life after death. The psalmist notes how experience appears to conflict with the doctrine of retribution.

> *Such are the wicked;*
> > *always at ease, they increase in riches.*
> *All in vain I have kept my heart clean*
> > *and washed my hands in innocence (vss. 12–13).*

But in the end the doctrine holds true. Wicked ways are ultimately punished.

> *But when I thought how to understand this,*
> > *it seemed to me a wearisome task,*
> *until I went into the sanctuary of God;*
> > *then I perceived their end.*
> *Truly you set them in slippery places;*
> > *you make them fall to ruin.*
> *How they are destroyed in a moment,*
> > *swept away utterly by terrors! (vss. 16–19)*

It took however a deeper and more intimate association with God to accept the wisdom of divine plans.

> *When my soul was embittered,*
> > *when I was pricked in heart,*
> *I was stupid and ignorant;*
> > *I was like a brute beast toward you.*

> *Nevertheless I am continually with you;*
>   *you hold my right hand.*
> *You guide me with your counsel,*
>   *and afterward you will receive me with honor.*
> *My flesh and my heart may fail,*
>   *but God is the strength of my heart and my portion*
>   *forever (vss. 21–24, 26).*

THE GLORIES OF NATURE

Psalm 148 beautifully illustrates how all creation reflects the glory of God. Such a prayer, deeply said and felt, can enhance a sense of responsibility for the continued beauty of the earth.

> *Praise the Lord from the earth,*
>   *you sea monsters and all deeps,*
> *Mountains and all hills,*
>   *fruit trees and all cedars!*
> *Wild animals and all cattle,*
>   *creeping things and flying birds! (vss 7, 9–10)*

All the faithful, all those close to God, should join in this adulation of the divine majesty (vss 13–14).

ALL PRAISE TO GOD

Psalm 150, the last of the book, is a typical hymn of praise. God is to be glorified in ritual and in personal awe before the heavens.

> *Praise the Lord!*
> *Praise God in his sanctuary;*
>   *praise him in his mighty firmament! (vs 1)*

For God is unique and has proven power.

> *Praise him for his mighty deeds;*
>   *praise him according to his surpassing greatness! (vs. 2)*

A variety of instruments should provide the music for a dance of praise (vss. 3–5) so that all living creatures may give God glory.

> *Let everything that breathes praise the LORD!*
> *Praise the LORD! (vs. 6)*

The upbeat ending brings to a culmination a variety of prayers in a variety of tones, both bright and somber — testimonies of a faith that despite all turmoil remains optimistic.

EGO–CONFIDENCE AND SELF–SUBMISSION

The optimism of the books of Proverbs and Psalms hardly results from ego-confidence. Security rooted in the ego alone would indicate a disposition quite foreign to the biblical sense of healthy self-will. Looking into Genesis, we can regard Jacob's determination as admirable because it is inevitably linked with *overtaking* God. What Jacob takes on is God's will, not overtaking it in the sense of subduing it, but in the sense of catching up with it. Optimism, linked with self-confidence of this kind, is always the correlate or partner of trust in God. In probing biblical views of religiousness, this should not be overlooked. The Bible's Psalms and Proverbs contribute to this theme over and over again, as Psalm 8 does for example in celebrating humanity's majestic or angelic power over nature.

Here the Psalms join hands with the New Age in proclaiming human responsibility for nature and the environment. The ecological interests of the New Age are part of a vision in which the right relationship of humanity to nature is part of spiritual maturity. The self attuned to nature is a self at one with the ultimate and holy power by which the earth and all creation moves toward greater beauty and harmony. The Psalms profess repeatedly that the person praying with a heart open to God can catch divine glory in nature and know in awe and humility what power over that creation human beings enjoy.

As introspective and mood-laden as they are, the Psalms consistently present a self that is essentially relational, that is constituted in dialogical partnership with God.[2] Psalm 8 does not look back to the Paradise of Eden, but rejoices that at the present moment God-given dignity and dominion are effective in humanity.[3]

In stressing personal diligence and industriousness, the Proverbs never lose sight of God as the ultimate trainer for the profitable life, the life of wisdom. As the Psalms put it, God is always and mightily, from a rejoicing heart and in all of nature, to be praised.

The psalmist's joy in engaging all of nature in the praise of God appears to imitate wisdom literature of ancient Egypt and reveals a faith that sees God's dominion reflected not only in humans but in every element of creation.[4] Praise of God, as a response to the divine source of all life, is necessarily the context and legitimation of human dominion over nature.[5]

The glory of God seen in nature can be related to the New Age view whereby divine power or energy suffuses all things. Such energy, even as a kind of consciousness or intelligence, is said to be found in crystals. So an appreciation of jewels and other types of crystalline stones can go far beyond the enjoyment of their beauty to the eye. The Psalms recount that Israel's king wore a crown (Ps 89:39; 132:18) that shone with gold and contained "a precious stone" (2 Sm 12:30). The high priest too wore such a crown at the Lord's command (Lv 8:9). Crowns like these have been appreciated in many ages and cultures as means of enhancing the power and consciousness of the wearer.[6] In Israel the priest also wore a breast-plate with twelve "stones . . . set in gold filigree" (Ex 28:17–20).

A faith attuned to God's resplendence might not fail to under-stand that divine guidance for Israel's kings and priests can be ampli-fied through the ornaments of the crown, through the jewels of God's creation. In a later age, a Christian vision of the New Jerusalem would include a wide variety of precious crystalline stones that adorn the foundation of that heavenly city (Rv 21:19–20).

The Bible's anthropology — or view of human nature — that links self-development with submission to God, and that makes fulfilled human existence entirely dependent on God,[7] blends well with New Age views of higher consciousness. Here there is a great deal of room for self-determination, assertion that in fact influ-ences the outcome of realities in one's world. For the Psalms deal not only with subjectivity or selfhood but also and emphatically with the effects of changed subjectivity on history.[8] Prayer has the power to alter circumstances. In a New Age perspective, self-deter-mination is no banal or ordinary manipulation of things, no merely egoistic power play. It is a matter of true autonomy that comes with developing spiritually by enhanced identity with the divine or God.[9] It is the kind of ruling that includes accord with the nonempirical powers by which things are brought to their proper ends. It means not trying to do everything alone but moving within the creative power of the divine.[10] This linking of two realms is a paradox, but as much for the Bible as for the New Age. It is the old paradox of destiny and freedom working hand in hand. It is the paradox at play in the prayer of petition. Believing God knows and plans whatever is to come, one may still pray to God, believing that such prayer influences the future that God already foresees.

TRUST'S LARGER VISION

Appreciating the paradox of destiny and freedom, the Proverbs do not simply advocate leaving everything to God. They also counsel justice, patience, calmness, and advice-seeking — virtues that require turning from one's simple ego demands and actively appreciating sources of higher wisdom in oneself as well as others. Thus the ant rather than the lazybones or sluggard is presented as the model of the wise.[11] The Psalms claim that compassion brings one a certain immunity from harm. This may be viewed as a specific application of the general principle appreciated by the Psalms, that spiritual development influences physical health. Sickness and guilt, healing and spirituality go hand in hand, and with them right relationships with others.[12] The Bible thus asserts that the terrain on which God's will is revealed and worked out is often larger than meets the ego's eye. This is something the New Age knows too. The basic divinity of human consciousness, in its view, is no dispensation from the ego's other basic need to look — for its own good — to something much larger than itself. Such looking is part of growth in consciousness and of realizing how concern for oneself includes concern for the good of all.

As mentioned earlier, the part or dimension of the person, insofar as she or he is in contact with the greater, life-giving whole, is what, from a New Age perspective, can be called the self. Progress toward fullness of the self can be inhibited by acts or attitudes that further enmesh one in the ego's world. On the other hand, this progress can be accelerated by acts or attitudes that further free one from the ego's world. The inhibition or retardation and the acceleration or facilitation follow with a certain naturalness from the kind of choices that one makes. It is a choice for slavery or freedom, deciding to stay trapped in negativity or to unlock one's inner doors to new and healthful possibilities. The position one takes brings with it punishments or rewards.

REWARD AND PUNISHMENT

The Bible looks at this dynamic in terms of the doctrine of retribution, a prominent notion throughout the Psalms and capsulized by Psalm 1 in the style of Israel's wisdom tradition.[13] Because, as the psalmist and other biblical authors note, the good often suffer and the malicious often enjoy good things, this doctrine is not presented simplistically. As a whole the Bible recognizes that the application of the doctrine must be quite nuanced or adjusted to the specific circumstances of individual cases. Psalm 73 portrays the antithesis of a naive faith not thoroughly tested. Mature faith, lived boldly in supportive fellowship with God, avoids cynicism in face of apparently unjust thriving or seemingly unjust suffering.[14]

The Bible thus appears to me to go further than the New Age in this regard. Though the New Age would want to conjoin personal misery with unenlightened consciousness, it would appear to have a hard time accepting that a truly just person can suffer.[15] At the most, it would see suffering as a kind of jolt to move a person into higher consciousness[16] or as a valuable opportunity for transition to a fuller life.[17] It can however regard the consideration of others' needs, rather than self-fulfillment, as a kind of sacrifice.[18] Acceptance of one's newer life can involve the sacrificial release of anyone or anything that blocks the way to higher consciousness.[19] The New Age is consistent in noting that destiny for ill or good is linked with the ill or good of one's choices in life. What is encouraging about the view is that the linkage is assumed to include hope for improvement. One is not permanently condemned to suffer for bad decisions or deeds, even if one must seek improvement in a future life, namely through a process of reincarnation.

The Psalms seem in no way to speak of any additional earthly life beyond that into which one is born. Yet they are confident in proclaiming that God's forgiveness, as a renewed and fortifying chance for new life, can always be expected. And they seem to show enthusiastically, as apparent in Psalm 73, that whatever justice is not experienced in this life will, by the judgment of God, be enjoyed in a heavenly life beyond death.[20] It is therefore not wise to judge life by transitory appearances. For God is permanently trustworthy, faithful, and just.[21] For the psalmist singing choruses of praise, there is every reason for extraordinary happiness.[22]

In looking at Genesis, I suggested that God's unrelenting willingness to forgive, even after many generations of sin, could be compared with the flexibility presumed by the principles involved in a New Age view of reincarnation. In looking at the Bible's Proverbs and Psalms, I would suggest that the doctrine of retribution can be added to the comparison. For in a New Age view of reincarnation, reward and punishment flow respectively, and with great strictness, toward responsible and irresponsible individuals. In this perspective, as in the perspective of the doctrine of retribution, they are given what they deserve.

Heightened Images

New Age interests are further paralleled in Proverbs and Psalms by appeal to the imagination and "right brain." In Genesis, as noted earlier, vibrant images like the burning torch and split animal carcasses are used. Pictures such as these enhance the impact of the scene where Abram makes a covenant with God. Images of the lazybones and the fruitful tree, only two of hundreds of such pictures in Proverbs and Psalms, work similarly. Appeal to the "right brain" is further sustained, especially in the Psalms, by the wide range of emotions that are given expression and provoked. The Psalms, with their awareness of the characteristic manner by which they sing and praise, appear to be quite conscious of the power of poetry[23] and imagery. Reliance on such power is by no means an exclusive characteristic of Psalms and Proverbs, however. Whether speaking historically or symbolically, the whole Bible, though less in works like Paul's epistles, uses pictorial presentations to make its points. Like the New Age, the Bible knows the limits of abstract, linear communication and succeeds in supplementing such messages with the graphics of picture and image.

Notes

1. Roland E. Murphy, *The Tree of Life: An Exploration of Biblical Wisdom Literature* (New York: Doubleday, 1990), 15–16, 125.

2. Harold Fisch, *Poetry with a Purpose: Biblical Poetics and Interpretation* (Bloomington, IN: Indiana University, 1988), 107–9.

3. Hans-Joachim Kraus, *Psalms 1–59: A Commentary*, trans. Hilton C. Oswald (Minneapolis: Augsburg, 1988), 185, 187.

4. Hans-Joachim Kraus, *Psalms 60–160*, trans. Hilton C. Oswald (Minneapolis: Augsburg, 1989), 562–64.

5. Walter Brueggemann, *The Message of the Psalms* (Minneapolis: Augsburg, 1984), 37–38, 165.

6. Randall N. Baer and Vicki Vittitow Baer, *The Crystal Connection: A Guidebook for Personal and Planetary Ascension* (San Francisco: Harper, 1987), 88–90, 171, 238.

7. Hans-Joachim Kraus, *Theology of the Psalms*, trans. Keith Crim (Minneapolis: Augsburg, 1986), 144, 150.

8. Fisch, *Poetry*, 109–11.

9. Joseph Chilton Pearce, *Magical Child Matures* (New York: Dutton, 1985), 139–42.

10. Carey, *Bird Tribes*, 56–59.

11. McKane, *Proverbs*, 323–24.

12. Kraus, *Psalms 1–59*, 433.

13. Mitchell Dahood, *Psalms I. 1–50: The Anchor Bible* (Garden City, NY: Doubleday, 1966), 1.

14. Brueggemann, *Message of the Psalms*, 116–21.

15. *Course in Miracles*, 76.

16. Dean H. Shapiro, Jr., "A Content Analysis of Eastern and Western Approaches to Therapy, Health, and Healing" in *Beyond Health and Normality: Explorations of Exceptional Psychological Well-being*, eds. Roger Walsh and Dean H. Shapiro (New York: Van Nostrand, 1983), 462–63.

17. Christina Grof and Stanislav Grof, *The Stormy Search for Self: A Guide to Personal Growth through Transformational Crises* (Los Angeles: Tarcher, 1990).

18. Ram Dass, *Grist for the Mill*, 32–33.
19. Carey, *Terra Christa*, 203–5.
20. Mitchell Dahood, *Psalms II. 51–100: The Anchor Bible* (Garden City, NY: Doubleday, 1968), 192, 196.
21. Kraus, *Psalms 60–150*, 91–93.
22. Brueggemann, *Message of the Psalms*, 167.
23. Fisch, *Poetry*, 119–20.

CHAPTER 5

The Parental
Face of Wisdom

Sirach 2–6, 16, 17, 27–31, 34, 37–39, 43, 48

THE LEARNED TEACHER

Jesus Ben Sira, the author of the Book of Sirach, was of the upper class and quite learned, quoting from or paraphrasing Greek and even Egyptian literature. Apparently written in the second century B.C.E., the book is not explicitly aimed at disputing with the foreign ideas that influenced but sometimes troubled his own people. He simply recounts Israel's heritage in his personalized manner and, from the foreign sources, adapts without fear what is useful or edifying for the established faith in which he was a devout participant.[1] His book, called Ecclesiasticus in some older translations, resembles the Book of Proverbs in that it contains many ideas and themes of both an everyday and philosophical nature.

Sirach is regarded as apocryphal by Protestants, which means that for these Christians the book is not, strictly speaking, part of the Bible though it is highly regarded among them as an inspirational work that harmonizes with the Bible's Wisdom literature. For Ben Sira the doctrine of retribution is very important, and he discusses it displaying admirable familiarity with the earlier books of Hebrew Scripture.[2] But some of the book's other distinctive themes will be emphasized here.

TRUST THROUGH ADVERSITY

Serving the Lord, a primary source of wisdom, is difficult and requires steadfastness and trust, no matter how trying the circumstances. Ben Sira, in the tradition of Wisdom writers, frequently addresses his disciple in a parental way. He offers support, encouragement, and firm directions.

> *My child, when you come to serve the LORD,*
> *prepare yourself for testing.*
> *Set your heart right and be steadfast,*
> *and do not be impetuous in time of adversity.*
> *Cling to him and do not depart,*
> *so that your last days will be prosperous.*
> *Accept whatever befalls you,*
> *in times of humiliation be patient.*
> *For gold is tested in the fire,*
> *and those found acceptable, in the furnace of*
> *humiliation.*
> *Trust in him, and he will help you;*
> *make your ways straight, and hope in him.*
> *Let us fall into the hands of the LORD,*
> *but not into the hands of mortals . . . (2:1–6, 17).*

Here the sage makes clear that suffering need not be viewed simply as punishment for sins. It is also a part of life as a testing place, as a crucible of refinement.

CARE FOR THOSE IN NEED

Almsgiving is a religious act of atonement and a reminder of responsibility for the good of others.

> *As water extinguishes a blazing fire,*
> *so almsgiving atones for sins.*
> *Those who repay favors give thought to the future;*
> *when they fall they will find support.*
> *My child, do not cheat the poor of their living,*
> *and do not keep needy eyes waiting.*

Do not grieve the hungry,
*   or anger one in need.*
Do not add to the troubles of the desperate,
*   or delay giving to the needy.*
Do not reject a suppliant in distress,
*   or turn your face away from the poor (3:30–4:4).*

Like the compassion mentioned in the psalms, generosity of this sort is also a safeguard against evil.

Store up almsgiving in your treasury,
*   and it will rescue you from every disaster;*
better than a stout shield and a sturdy spear,
*   it will fight for you against the enemy (29:12–13).*

For wealth is unreliable and offers no protection should God's wrathful judgment be the fitting response to sin.

Do not rely on your wealth,
*   or say, 'I have enough.'*
Do not depend on dishonest wealth,
*   for it will not benefit you on the day of calamity (5:1, 8).*

CLEAN AND UNCLEAN LIPS

Likewise speech should be used only for the good of others.

Honor and dishonor come from speaking,
*   and the tongue of mortals may be their downfall.*
Do not be called double-tongued,
*   and do not lay traps with your tongue;*
for shame comes to the thief,
*   and severe condemnation to the double-tongued.*
In great and small matters cause no harm,
*   and do not become an enemy instead of a friend;*
for a bad name incurs shame and reproach . . . (5:13–6:1).

Ben Sira's concern for proper speech is elaborated later in the book when he observes that a person's speech is a revelation of that person's character.

When a sieve is shaken, the refuse appears;
    so do a person's faults when he speaks.
The kiln tests the potter's vessels;
    so the test of a person is in his conversation.
Its fruit discloses the cultivation of a tree;
    so a person's speech discloses the cultivation of his
        mind (27:4–6).

The sage observes how disturbing quarrelsomeness is.

Refrain from strife, and your sins will be fewer;
    for the hot-tempered kindle strife,
and the sinner disrupts friendships
    and sows discord among those who are at peace (28:8–9).

Speech then can either be a sign of virtue or a sign of vice. A troublesome tongue can weaken others, making them vulnerable to various evil influences, and disrupting their lives.

If you blow on a spark, it will glow;
    if you spit on it, it will be put out;
        yet both come out of your mouth!
Curse the gossips and the double-tongued,
    for they destroy the peace of many.
Slander has shaken many,
    and scattered them from nation to nation;
it has destroyed strong cities,
    and overturned the houses of the great.
Slander has driven virtuous women from their homes, and
    deprived them of the fruit of their toil (28:12–15).

Speech can even be irreversibly destructive. The old adage, that only sticks and stones hurt, does not always hold.

The blow of a whip raises a welt,
    but a blow of the tongue crushes the bones.
Many have fallen by the edge of the sword,
    but not as many as have fallen because of the tongue
        (28:17–18).

One's speech then can be very powerful and horrible.

> For its yoke is a yoke of iron,
>> and its fetters are fetters of bronze;
> its death is an evil death,
>> and Hades is preferable to it (28:20–21).

Horrid speech is not a characteristic of the just but marks well and destroys those who are malicious.

> It has no power over the godly;
>> they will not be burned in its flame.
> Those who forsake the LORD will fall into its power;
>> it will burn among them and will not be put out.
> It will be sent out against them like a lion;
>> like a leopard it will mangle them (28:22–23).

Here Sirach teaches that speech is not only expressive of character but also formative of it. For, as he later points out, one's understanding and outlook determine actions and are intimately conjoined with the way one speaks.

> Discussion is the beginning of every work,
>> and cousel precedes every undertaking.
> The mind is the root of all conduct;
>> it sprouts four branches,
> good and evil, life and death;
>> and it is the tongue that continually rules them (37:16–18).

So one should be on guard.

> As you fence in your property with thorns,
>> so make a door and a bolt for your mouth.
> As you lock up your silver and gold,
>> so make balances and scales for your words.
> Take care not to err with your tongue,
>> and fall victim to one lying in wait (28:24–26).

Discourse on the power of the tongue reveals poignantly how body, mind, and spirit are conjoined.

WHOLENESS AND HEALTH

But there are other ways by which Ben Sira expounds on the relationship of body, mind, and spirit. First of all good health and positive emotions go hand in hand. Joy and gladness are life-giving and facilitate the body's response to nutrients.

> *There is no wealth better than health of body,*
>   *and no gladness above joy of heart.*
> *A joyful heart is life itself,*
>   *and rejoicing lengthens one's life span.*
> *Those who are cheerful and merry at table*
>   *will benefit from their food (30:16, 22, 25).*

So bitterness, negativity, resentment, worry, envy, and anger are a burden to health and can even bring one to the grave.

> *Death is better than a life of misery,*
>   *and eternal sleep than chronic sickness.*
> *Do not give yourself over to sorrow,*
>   *and do not distress yourself deliberately.*
> *Distract yourself and take comfort,*
>   *and remove sorrow far from you,*
> *for sorrow has destroyed many,*
>   *and no advantage ever comes from it.*
> *Jealousy and anger shorten life,*
>   *and anxiety brings on premature old age (30:17, 21, 23–24).*

Like wealth, food has its dangers, being able to bring discomfort as well as disturbed sleep.

> *Eat what is set before you like a well brought-up person,*
>   *and do not chew greedily. . . .*
> *The distress of sleeplessness and of nausea*
>   *and colic are with the glutton (31:16, 20b).*

Something similar can be said of drink, which can contribute to healthy merriment or induce destructive feelings.

> Do not try to prove your strength by wine-drinking,
> for wine has destroyed many.
> As the furnace tests the work of the smith,
> so wine tests hearts when the insolent quarrel.
> Wine is very life to human beings
> if taken in moderation.
> What is life to one who is without wine?
> It has been created to make people happy.
> Wine drunk at the proper time and in moderation
> is rejoicing of heart and gladness of soul.
> Wine drunk to excess leads to bitterness of spirit,
> to quarrels and stumbling (31:25–29).

Moderation needs however to be combined with the greatest balm to body, mind, and spirit, namely authentic religiousness.

> The eyes of the LORD are on those who love him,
> a mighty shield and strong support,
> a shelter from scorching wind and a shade from noonday sun,
> a guard against stumbling and a help against falling.
> He lifts up the soul and makes the eyes sparkle;
> He gives health and life and blessing (34:19–20).

At times however one may have recourse to a physician, an appropriate step since it profits from the physician's divinely given skills on which one should rely, though always in conjunction with firm religious faith. Such piety is required of the physician as well as the patient.

> Honor physicians for their services. . . .
> for their gift of healing comes from the Most High. . . .
> And he gave skill to human beings
> that he might be glorified in his marvelous works.
> By them the physician heals and takes away pain; . . .
> My child, when you are ill, do not delay,
> but pray to the LORD, and he will heal you.
> Then give the physician his place, for the LORD created him;
> do not let him leave you, for you need him.

> *There may come a time when recovery lies in the hands of physicians,*
> *for they too pray to the LORD*
> *that he grant them success in diagnosis*
> *and in healing, for the sake of preserving life (38:1–2, 6–7, 9,*
> *12–14).*

EVALUATING PARANORMAL PHENOMENA

We have observed a respect for dreams, visions, and prophecies in the stories of Jacob and Joseph. Here Ben Sira exhibits skepticism toward reliance on phenomena of the paranormal since they are often illusory and not the result of God's influence. Indulging in them can be foolhardy and even fatal.

> *The senseless have vain and false hopes,*
> *and dreams give wings to fools.*
> *As one who catches at a shadow and pursues the wind,*
> *so is anyone who believes in dreams.*
> *What is seen in dreams is but a reflection,*
> *the likeness of a face looking at itself.*
> *From an unclean thing what can be clean?*
> *And from something false what can be true?*
> *Divinations and omens and dreams are unreal,*
> *and like a woman in labor, the mind has fantasies.*
> *Unless they are sent by intervention from the Most High,*
> *pay no attention to them.*
> *For dreams have deceived many,*
> *and those who put their hope in them have perished (34:1–7).*

Such a view accords with that of the Book of Deuteronomy. In both cases, however, it should be observed that a major part of the condemnation has to do with the idolatry the biblical authors see connected with such phenomena. What is decisive here is commitment to the God of Israel. *Any* practice that detracts from such faith is reprehensible. Even prophecy, a paranormal form of disclosing God's word and an institution well established in Israel, is intolerable if it is not connected with the Lord as known according to this people's faith.[3]

> *When you come into the land that the* LORD *your God is giving you,*
> *you must not learn to imitate the abhorrent practices of those*
> *nations. No one shall be found among you who makes a son or*
> *daughter pass through fire, or who practices divination, or is a sooth-*
> *sayer, or an augur, or a sorcerer, or one who casts spells, or who con-*
> *sults ghosts or spirits, or who seeks oracles from the dead. For who-*
> *ever does these things is abhorrent to the* LORD; *it is because of such*
> *abhorrent practices that the* LORD *your God is driving them out*
> *before you. You must remain completely loyal to the* LORD *your God.*
> *Although these nations that you are about to dispossess do give heed*
> *to soothsayers and diviners, as for you, the* LORD *your God does not*
> *permit you to do so. . . . But any prophet who speaks in the name of*
> *other gods, or who presumes to speak in my name a word that I*
> *have not commanded the prophet to speak — that prophet shall die*
> (Dt 18:9–14, 20).

This accords with Hebrew Scripture's general disposition toward
paranormal awareness. The work of diviners, seers, and other personalities who could discern what is ordinarily hidden was recognized by biblical writers as reliable even among those who practiced other religions. In Israel however such gifts were accepted
only when they were used in the service of Israel's faith.[4]

Clearly, both Sirach and Deuteronomy teach that the origins
of paranormal phenomena must be discerned. Distinguishing the
edifying from the dangerous, says Sirach, requires broad experience and dedicated religiousness.

> *An educated person knows many things,*
> *and one with much experience knows what he is talking*
> *about.*
> *The spirit of those who fear the* LORD *will live,*
> *for their hope is in him who saves them.*
> *Those who fear the* LORD *will not be timid,*
> *or play the coward, for he is their hope.*
> *Happy is the soul that fears the* LORD (34:9, 14–17)!

In the matter of discernment Ben Sira is more skeptical of advice-
seeking than was the author of Proverbs.

Be wary of a counselor,
and learn first what is his interest,
for he will take thought for himself.
He may cast the lot against you (37:8).

ONESELF AS A SOURCE OF TRUTH

More important are companions who likewise seek God's truth. In such a context one can eminently trust one's own heart.

But associate with a godly person
whom you know to be a keeper of the commandments,
who is like-minded with yourself,
and who will grieve with you if you fail.
And heed the counsel of your own heart,
for no one is more faithful to you than it is.
For our own mind sometimes keeps us better informed than
seven sentinels sitting high on a watchtower.
But above all pray to the Most High
that he may direct your way in truth (37:12–15).

For Ben Sira then the personal pursuit of wisdom is life's highest goal.

A wise person will have praise heaped upon him,
and all who see him will call him happy.
One who is wise among his people will inherit honor,
and his name will live forever (37:24, 26).

HELPS TO WISDOM

Such an achievement requires a certain amount of leisure. For to know the ways of God, the wise person must, besides looking within, study the tradition and the great masters.

How different the one who devotes himself
to the study of the law of the Most High!

> *He seeks out the wisdom of all the ancients,*
> > *and is concerned with prophecies;*
> *he preserves the sayings of the famous*
> > *and penetrates the subtleties of parables;*
> *he seeks out the hidden meanings of proverbs*
> > *and is at home with the obscurities of parables*
> > > *(38:34b–39:3).*

Humble prayer and attentive meditation are also necessary.

> *He sets his heart to rise early*
> > *to seek the LORD who made him,*
> > *and to petition the Most High;*
> *He opens his mouth in prayer,*
> > *and asks pardon for his sins.*
> *If the great LORD is willing,*
> > *he will be filled with the spirit of understanding;*
> *he will pour forth words of wisdom of his own*
> > *and give thanks to the LORD in prayer.*
> *The LORD will direct his counsel and knowledge,*
> > *as he meditates on his mysteries (39:5–7).*

True Joy

In sharing this wisdom with others, a rewarding wisdom that comes from God, the wise person will enjoy unending praise.

> *He will show the wisdom of what he has learned,*
> > *and will glory in the law of the LORD's covenant.*
> *Many will praise his understanding;*
> > *it will never be blotted out.*
> *His memory will not disappear,*
> > *and his name will live through all generations (39:8–9).*

The contentment that comes with such fame will reach its fullness when the wise person finds the goodness of God in all things, even those at first not welcomed, and praises God accordingly.

All the works of the LORD are good,
and he will supply every need in its time.
No one can say, 'This is not as good as that,'
for everything proves good in its appointed time.
So now sing praise with all your heart and voice,
and bless the name of the LORD (39:33–35).

SPEECH AND HIGHER CONSCIOUSNESS

The Book of Sirach is a particularly rich collection of teachings that allow a comparison of the Bible's Wisdom tradition with the tenets of the New Age. The sage Ben Sira who originally wrote the book's impressive instructions knew of the ways and thought patterns typical of the Hellenistic or Greek-speaking society of which his world was a part. His chief interest was in reminding his readers of the great wealth the Hebrew traditions held for them. Many of the perspectives he offered would be further developed in the Christian Scripture two to three centuries later. His originality of expression and his sensitivity to human behavior well allowed him to depict avidly the power of human consciousness.

Ben Sira's way of carrying forward the biblical theme of trust is closely connected with his vision of such power. He dwells on the relevance of speech since he appreciates it as something that is far more than a means of communication between persons. What one says is both an indicator and generator of what one is. According to Sirach this means that speech expresses and influences attitudes, and attitudes are modes of consciousness that influence feelings and behavior. Disruptive, insulting, or belittling speech can truly harm other people. The abusive language enters their minds, helps to distort their thoughts, and thus brings harm to them, even bodily harm. Negativity in thought, Ben Sira suggests, can lead to negative behavior and physical illness.

But abuse through such speech is also heaped on the speaker. Utterances orient a person's mind and feelings. For good or ill, they affect character, whether they are about oneself or about others. One does well then to speak kindly as much as possible. For this brings both relief and refreshment to one's spirit.

To quarrel is to induce strife and division, even between the closest friends. But it is also to poison the life of the quarreller, who is usually the person the squabble was assumed would help. In such a case the troublesome words not only cause the hearer trouble, but affect what the speaker sees, namely strife. The more the speaker holds forth without listening, the more appropriate it seems to argue. Noting the relationship between truth and one's inner dispositions, the New Age can look at the speaker's predicament as an example of truth being constituted from within. A speaker with a changed message, like a singer with a different tune, will see another situation and so another truth. Negative speech is a sign and instigator of faulty consciousness. How reasonable it is then to abide in speech that is positive, pleasant, supportive, or edifying.

> *The mind is the root of all conduct;*
> *it sprouts four branches,*
> *good and evil, life and death;*
> *and it is the tongue that continually rules them*
> *(37:17–18).*

The influence of speech on thoughts that in turn affect feelings and behavior is depicted by Ben Sira in such a way that a parallel between elements of the Bible's Wisdom literature and current psychology's cognitive therapy becomes clear. The New Age approach to consciousness, as already observed, can be closely aligned with this method of psychotherapy whereby positive cognitions or thoughts are understood as the primary ingredients of mental health. The parallel becomes even clearer when one takes into account alternate ways by which the Wisdom literature sees the relationship between speech, thoughts, and happiness. If Ben Sira viewed the relationship as starting more or less with speech, the sage who authored the Book of Proverbs helps one to understand too that the relationship can start with cognitions:

> *The mind of the wise makes their speech judicious,*
> *and adds persuasiveness to their lips.*
> *Pleasant words are like a honeycomb,*
> *sweetness to the soul and health to the body (16:23–24).*

Here, with the starting point in the mind, speech's influence is seen as flowing directly to the soul or psyche and to the body. The sages thus allow us to conclude that profitable dispositions can begin with either positive statements or positive cognitions since the influence of word and thought is reciprocal. Such interaction can likely be associated with the body as well, which would be the reason why, in Ben Sira's total vision of contentment or blessedness, he includes moderation in the enjoyment of food and drink. Edifying speech, constructive thoughts, and a healthy body are mutually beneficial. Not to attend to them, suggests the sage, is foolish.

TOTAL HEALTH

Today, in line with New Age holistic approaches to health, medical professionals are increasingly aware of the power of their words — for good or ill — in treatment, surgery, and recovery. Clearly, discouraging words are to be avoided; and encouraging, supportive words are to be highly recommended. For the patient will frequently respond in accord with them, sometimes in contrast with physical indications of ability to do so.[5]

The positive emotions that can result from higher consciousness are of great interest to Ben Sira. For they too affect the person who exhibits them. They induce good physical health and longer life. Negative emotions have the opposite effect; their influence is deadening. Even in the most adverse of times one should strive patiently to exhibit trust in the sustaining and renewing presence of divine energies. The New Age looks on negative dispositions such as bitterness, resentment, and worry as counterproductive in the maintenance of health and in the process of heightening one's consciousness. Conversely, positive dispositions such as love, hope, and humor have an enormously beneficial impact on one's bodily condition.[6] Here the holistic view of human health — in the unity of body, mind, and spirit — plays a major role on the journey where the divinity of one's consciousness is realized.

In line with biblical anthropology — the sacred texts' views of human nature — Sirach does not regard the wise person as divine.

The book does, however, assume a holistic stance toward health and wholeness. All aspects of human life, including attention to diet, are part of cultivating wisdom. For the health of the body can be intimately linked with the health of the mind and spirit. Fullness of life means wholeness of humanity. Sirach's link between humanity and divinity is presented as an intimate relationship between wisdom and authentic religiousness. Thus it would agree with the New Age that the power of the divine is necessary for joy, fulfillment, and good health.

In surmounting times of sickness, such power is necessary for both the healed and the healer. Ben Sira is perhaps more trustful of physicians than other biblical authors. Yet in accord with traditional biblical faith, he places healing ultimately in the hands of God. The physicians Ben Sira knew did not of course have the scientific training that is characteristic of present-day medicine, but they were trained in the scientific methods of healing that had developed in the Hellenistic or Greek world with which Israel of the time was in contact.[7] Nor do they seem to have been shamans, holistic promoters of health who have attracted the attention of the New Age.

Found worldwide and throughout history, these healers are able to induce astounding transformations in their patients through altered states of consciousness, through their own brands of psychotherapy, through suggestion, and through apparently paranormal influence.[8] However Ben Sira saw in physicians a potential to facilitate healing through knowledge acquired with God's help and through the spiritual power of prayer. This view of healing, along with Ben Sira's sensitivity to the power of words, displays much resemblance with the New Age approach to healing. Here cures for the body, which is holistically one with the mind and spirit, are thought to profit from psychological and spiritual influences at least as much as from physical ones.[9]

DIVINATION AND SUCH

Ben Sira's respect for spiritual power does not include pronounced approval of what we today call the paranormal. In Genesis, Laban and Joseph speak quite respectfully of divination or fortune-telling. Ben Sira's caution in the matter finds support however in other

parts of the Bible, for example in Deuteronomy. Such ambiva-
lence or inconsistency is linked with the Bible's exclusivism
regarding biblical faith as a path of true religion. We have seen
this in the opening chapters of Genesis where it is suggested that
Gentile gods are deficient compared with the God of Israel. From
this perspective there is only one fully approvable path toward
God.

In ancient Israel practices associated with the religions of other
peoples were even punishable by death. With religious faith at the
heart of the community's identity, such idolatrous practices in
Israel were analogous to espionage and treason. The loyalty that
was expected to exclude such foreign usage had its parallels in the
institutions of other peoples in ancient times.[10] But the case for the
Bible's religious exclusivism, it can be argued, is not open-and-
shut. For the depiction of the rainbow covenant in Genesis shows
God's great dedication to all peoples. Other parts of Hebrew and
Christian Scripture reflect respect for the ways of those who do
not fit snugly into general biblical categories of those who are chosen or saved:

> For from the rising of the sun to its setting my name is great among
> the nations, and in every place incense is offered to my name, and a
> pure offering; for my name is great among the nations, says the LORD
> of hosts (Mal 1:11).

> Now the woman was a Gentile, of Syrophoenician origin. She begged
> him [Jesus] to cast the demon out of her daughter. . . . So she went
> home, found the child lying on the bed, and the demon gone (Mk
> 7:26, 30).

> Ever since the creation of the world his eternal power and divine
> nature, invisible though they are, have been understood and seen
> through the things he has made. . . . For it is not the hearers of the law
> who are righteous in God's sight, but the doers of the law who will be
> justified. When Gentiles . . . do instinctively what the law requires,
> these, though not having the law, are a law to themselves. They show
> that what the law requires is written on their hearts. . . (Rom 1:20;
> 2:13–15).

Then Paul stood in front of the Areopagus and said, 'Athenians, I see
how extremely religious you are in every way. For as I went through
the city and looked carefully at the objects of your worship, I found
among them an altar with the inscription, "To an unknown god."
What therefore you worship as unknown, this I proclaim to you' (Acts
17:22–23).

Yet overall the Bible appears rather careful to depict true religion in terms of faith in the God of Israel, and more specifically
from the Christian stance, in the God of Jesus Christ. Here we see
one of the greatest disagreements between the Bible and the New
Age since the latter clearly and explicitly accepts that many paths to
the divine or to higher consciousness can be valid. Paranormal
activity may be part of any such path. The Bible appears to be more
restrictive, commending only those paranormal phenomena that
are part of what it presents as authentic religiousness. Here the
Bible is consistent. It is designed to ground and fashion persons in
a given religious tradition. We would thus not expect it to promote
nonbiblical religious activities any more than we would expect it to
promote other religions such as Hinduism or Confucianism. It
gives its attention wholly to the faith and religious traditions of
which it is a part.

That is why Sirach accepts the legitimacy of the biblical
prophets — whom the Bible claims were gifted by God with paranormal precognition, or unusual foreknowledge of the future — as
well as other paranormal powers. Sirach proudly recounts how
Elijah "raised a corpse from death" (48:5) and how wondrously
God had worked through a later prophet:

In Isaiah's days the sun went backward,
    and he prolonged the life of the king.
By his dauntless spirit he saw the future,
    and comforted the mourners in Zion (48:23–24).

One might suppose then that if other paranormal phenomena
could be accepted as vehicles by which persons are authentically
touched by divinity, Sirach too would be receptive to them. For the
point of wisdom is knowing God and recognizing divine designs.

This is at times a tedious process, at least one that takes great dedication. Much of it is accomplished by turning inward, not however
by unassumingly trusting in dreams. Here again Sirach exhibits
caution far less pronounced in other parts of the Bible, as in
Genesis where Joseph and his brothers display much confidence in
the power of dreams to reveal important truths. For Sirach, the
legitimacy of *anything* for true wisdom has to do with its origin. Do
not trust it unless it is "sent by intervention from the Most High"
(34:6), namely by God as known to Israel. And Sirach has made it
clear that study, consultation, and prayer are very important for
knowing what is of God. It seems there are no absolute rules for
knowing with certainty where God is or is not at work. It is a matter of discernment.

DETERMINING TRUTH

Yet the rules Ben Sira proposes are words to the wise, especially
the directive about turning to one's heart and conscience for guidance. The truth determined here is wisdom found because one's
heart and mind are set on God in a prayerful way.[11] A determination of this kind is highly reliable and quite different from the
schemes devised by prideful cunning. The New Age, in a parallel
way, would regard attainment of wisdom an accomplishment of the
self rather than the ego. For truth that emerges from the self is
reliable because the self is centered on the divine.

In conjoining speech, attitudes, and the situation of the
speaker, Sirach observes how everything is affected by the kind or
unkind words that are uttered.[12] This way of relating internal and
external elements to one another helps the wise person interpret
situations as effects of personal and internal dispositions. In linking
words with consciousness, the New Age sees in them tremendous
power to transform.[13] In contemporary physics it is shown how the
choices of observers or researchers significantly affect what they
find. The determination of truth in such situations is not merely
the finding of truth but in a certain way the constitution of truth,
the establishment of truth.

The Lord created human beings out of earth. . . .
He endowed them with strength like his own
      and made them in his own image . . .
      and gave them dominion over beasts and birds.
Discretion and tongue . . . he gave them (17:1a, 3, 4b, 6).

Persons made in the likeness of God may thus be imitating in their distinctive ways what God at creation did in naming or choosing the various elements of creation before they appeared. "God said, 'Let there be light'; and there was light" (Gn 1:3). Similar words brought forth the rest of creation.[14] One can argue that Sirach could not go much further in agreeing with the New Age that truth is constituted from within. One's thoughts and words do determine results.

For Sirach God is "all in all." Although the apparently original text can be rendered literally so that God is depicted simply as "the all" (43:27b), *all in all* here seems to capture Ben Sira's intent. Throughout his book he speaks of God as personal, praiseworthy, and "greater" (43:28b) than all creation.[15] This vision of the divine, present *in* every element of nature and the universe, does not appear to be the same as a New Age monism whereby everything is regarded *as* divine. The two views appear very close in light of the oneness they both depict between human consciousness and divine power.

For the New Age this oneness suggests: look at your life or world that you see lacking or hurting, and know that by a change in consciousness you can make it better, astoundingly better. For Sirach this oneness provides similar consolation and encouragement: look at your life or world that you see lacking or hurting, and know that by a change in consciousness you can make your very life better and thus improve your world. The essence of such consciousness appears to be participation in the divine wisdom that is everywhere at work, everywhere, in all things, no matter how things appear to the unwise, to the one the Wisdom literature calls the fool. The words of Sirach 39 are worth repeating:

All the works of the LORD are good,
      and he will supply every need in its time.
No one can say, 'This is not as good as that,'
      for everything proves good in its appointed time (vss 33–34).

From a New Age perspective the foolishness that painfully longs for what is not at hand, either because its time has passed or not yet come, is rooted in a needless feeling of attachment to something or someone thought to be indispensable. By a change of attitude, by accepting that a *preference* for the desired object is not the same as the *perceived need* for it, one can become free of the ceaseless longing and thus of the pain. Happiness then comes with enjoying what is present and in letting preferences become realities in due time, however distant such a time may be.[16] For the New Age, the divine essence is gracious and abundant, an unlimited source of wondrous gifts.[17] Through needless desires for what we think we need right now, we feel alone and deprived. With acceptance of immediate joys, we experience life as part of a friendly plan in which our real needs are at every moment met miraculously and abundantly.[18] Ben Sira's admonition, provoking trust in both God's timing[19] and God's abundance, echoes the famous words of Psalm 23 where the believer's confidence in God's goodness, in God's meeting every need both at present and in the future,[20] springs from a heart that knows intimacy with the divine:

> The LORD is my shepherd, I shall not want.
> Surely goodness and mercy shall follow me
>   all the days of my life,
> and I shall dwell in the house of the LORD
>   my whole life long (vss 1, 6).

For those filled with such trust, God provides abundant blessings, even in the midst of turmoil.[21] Words like these are no approval of, or cowardly concession to, the very real evil in the world. They are rather courageously religious proclamations that all can be born to one's advantage and comfort, even the greatest sorrows and defeats, because godly wisdom far surpasses any merely human fear.

Notes

1. Patrick W. Skehan and Alexander A. Di Lella, *The Wisdom of Ben Sira: The Anchor Bible* (New York: Doubleday, 1987), 16, 46–50, 452.
2. Murphy, *Tree of Life*, 74–76.
3. Gerhard von Rad, *Deuteronomy: A Commentary* (Philadelphia: Westminster, 1966), 123–25.
4. Eichrodt, *Old Testament*, 295–303.
5. Siegel, *Peace, Love and Healing*, 85–100.
6. Blair Justice, *Who Gets Sick: How Beliefs, Moods and Thoughts Affect Your Health* (Los Angeles: Tarcher, 1988), 255–72.
7. John G. Snaith, *Ecclesiasticus or The Wisdom of Jesus Son of Sirach* (Cambridge: Cambridge University, 1974), 184.
8. Walsh, *Spirit of Shamanism*, 159–204.
9. Capra, *Uncommon Wisdom*, 159, 175.
10. Peter C. Craigie, *The Book of Deuteronomy* (Grand Rapids, MI: Eerdmans, 1976), 59, 249–51.
11. Skehan and Di Lella, *Ben Sira*, 79, 433.
12. Skehan and Di Lella, *Ben Sira*, 436.
13. Karpinski, *Two Worlds*, 75, 210.
14. Fred Alan Wolf, *Parallel Universes: The Search for Other Worlds* (New York: Simon & Schuster, 1990), 179–80.
15. Skehan and Di Lella, *Ben Sira*, 495–96.
16. Ken Keyes, Jr., *Handbook to Higher Consciousness* (Coos Bay, OR: Love Line, 1975), 19–22.
17. Karpinski, *Two Worlds*, 37.
18. Keyes, *Higher Consciousness*, 68–70, 200.
19. Dianne Bergant, *What Are They Saying about Wisdom Literature?* (New York: Paulist, 1984), 70.
20. Brueggemann, *Message of the Psalms*, 155–56.
21. Carey, *Terra Christa*, 71–72.

CHAPTER 6

In the Fullness of Time

Luke 1–13, 17–19, 21, 24

A GOSPEL FOR THE GENTILES

The gospel named for the Greek-speaking Luke appears to have originated late in the first century. Luke wanted to assure the predominantly Gentile Christians that they were part of God's redemptive plan that had precedent in Judaism and was now being carried out under the guidance of the Holy Spirit[1]. The gospel talks about the beginnings of a new phase of the plan in the life and works of Jesus.

CALLED TO THE NEW

Full of the Spirit, Jesus prepared in the desert for his mission. Not material sustenance, nor power, nor the attractiveness of evil succeeded in tempting him from his calling. The devil

> took him to Jerusalem, and placed him on the pinnacle of the temple, saying to him, 'If you are the Son of God, throw yourself down from here' (4:9).

Jesus was not relying on God in a foolhardy manner but was deeply in tune with God's will. This does not mean the way would be easy for Jesus. The tempter would return.

111

When the devil had finished every test, he departed from him until an opportune time (4:13).

Jesus began his mission by observing that he was fulfilling the prophecy of Isaiah regarding the arrival of the final age (4:18–21). With this age, divine blessings would bring renewed and permanent freedom, along with healing and forgiveness. It would be what some call a "new age,"[2] though not in exactly the same sense that the modern "New Age" is so called. As part of the final age or biblical time of fulfillment, Jesus is portrayed by Luke as the primary agent of goodness. For many appeared in awe over the power of his speech as it went out in various settings to demons and to illnesses.

They were all amazed and kept saying to one another, 'What kind of utterance is this? For with authority and power he commands the unclean spirits, and out they come!' (4:36)

He stood over her and rebuked the fever, and it left her. Immediately she got up and began to serve them. As the sun was setting, all those who had any who were sick with various kinds of diseases brought them to him; and he laid his hands on each of them and cured them (4:39–40).

His powers over nature were displayed when he told Simon to lower the fishnets for a great catch:

When they had done this, they caught so many fish that their nets were beginning to break. So they signaled their partners in the other boat to come and help them. And they came and filled both boats, so that they began to sink (5:6–7).

Power such as this helped him attract disciples who would later continue his work.

They left everything and followed him (5:11).

CLOSENESS TO GOD

Jesus however was not a total activist but frequently took time for spiritual renewal.

He would withdraw to deserted places and pray (5:16).

Thus the power of God could work greatly through him.

> *One day, while he was teaching, Pharisees and teachers of the law were sitting near by (they had come from every village of Galilee and Judea and from Jerusalem); and the power of the LORD was with him to heal* (5:17).

One of his greatest powers however, one traditionally ascribed solely to God, was to forgive sins.

> *The scribes and the Pharisees began to question, . . . 'Who can forgive sins but God alone?' When Jesus perceived their questionings, he answered them, 'Why do you raise such questions in your hearts? . . . The Son of Man has authority on earth to forgive sins . . . '* (5:21–24).

The hearts of many can be changed. Therefore Jesus says,

> *'I have come to call not the righteous but sinners to repentance'* (5:32).

In light of this repentance, the kind of change that Jesus calls for is radical, involving a very high form of love and generosity: enemies must be loved and good must be done without expecting anything in return.

> *'I say to you that listen, Love your enemies, do good to those who hate you, bless those who curse you, pray for those who abuse you. If anyone strikes you on the cheek, offer the other also; . . . and lend, expecting nothing in return'* (6:27–29, 35).

Virtue like this may appear exorbitant to spiritually frail humans. By God's mighty ways it is routine. But, having been touched by divine forgiveness, disciples are in a position to be in fact more like the God in whose image they were made:

> *'You will be children of the Most High; for he is kind to the ungrateful and the wicked. Be merciful, just as your Father is merciful'* (6:35–36).

To act otherwise is to go against one's very nature as a child of God and thus to experience that hardness of heart has distressing consequences. Jesus thus exhorts,

> *'Do not judge, and you will not be judged; do not condemn, and you will not be condemned. Forgive, and you will be forgiven' (6:37).*

To act otherwise is foolishly to allow oneself to be misdirected. It is like, says Jesus in the imagery of a parable, the blind leading the blind (6:39). On the other hand, in traveling the route Jesus suggests, disciples not only imitate God but

> *'will be like the teacher' (6:40),*

namely like Jesus himself. That is why he calls for compassion and encourages his disciples to pray:

> *'Forgive us our sins,*
> *   for we ourselves forgive everyone indebted to us' (11:4).*

JESUS' WONDROUS POWERS

Jesus' own compassion extended to many, even to the dead; his life-giving power made clear to many more how the power of God was active in him.

> *He came forward and touched the bier, and the bearers stood still. And he said, 'Young man, I say to you, rise!' The dead man sat up and began to speak, and Jesus gave him to his mother. Fear seized all of them; and they glorified God, saying, 'A great prophet has risen among us!' and 'God has looked favorably on his people!' (7:14–16).*

On another occasion the person touched was a girl.

> *He took her by the hand and called out, 'Child , get up!' Her spirit returned, and she got up at once. Then he directed them to give her something to eat (8:54–55).*

With him the Messianic age had arrived.

> *And he answered them, 'Go and tell John what you have seen and heard: the blind receive their sight, the lame walk, the lepers are cleansed, the deaf hear, the dead are raised, the poor have good news brought to them' (7:22).*

And anyone who belongs to that new age or is born into God's kingdom is in a much more favorable position than even a prophet of the former age.

> *'I tell you, among those born of women, no one is greater than John; yet the least in the kingdom of God is greater than he' (7:28).*

Jesus' wondrous powers could go deeply within. Jesus could know a person's thoughts, read a person's heart, and offer the greatest mercy. On one occasion, when he was dining with a Pharisee, a woman

> *stood behind him at his feet, weeping, and began to bathe his feet with her tears ... Now when the Pharisee who had invited him saw it, he said to himself, 'If this man were a prophet, he would have known who and what kind of woman this is who is touching him — that she is a sinner.' Jesus spoke up and said to him, "Simon , I have something to say to you. .... Her sins, which were many, have been forgiven' (7:38–40, 47).*

The Disciples as Jesus' Kin

Jesus teaches in many ways that those responding to the word of God must display diligence, openness, and fruitfulness. They fit his famous parable where he used the imagery of sowing. Like the seed

> *'in the good soil, these are the ones who, when they hear the word, hold it fast in an honest and good heart, and bear fruit with patient endurance' (8:15).*

This sort of response, Jesus says, makes the disciples one of his kin:

> *'My mother and my brothers are those who hear the word of God and do it' (8:21).*

Relationship with Jesus however brings with it the responsibility of spreading the good news of his mission.

> *The man from whom the demons had gone begged that he might be with him; but Jesus sent him away, saying, 'Return to your home, and declare how much God has done for you.' So he went away, proclaiming throughout the city how much Jesus had done for him (8:38–39).*

With this kind of responsibility comes something awesome, the actual power to continue Jesus' mission itself, especially that of preaching and healing.

> *Jesus called the twelve together and gave them power and authority over all demons and to cure diseases, and he sent them out to proclaim the kingdom of God and to heal (9:1–2).*

The disciple thus participates in Jesus' mission to nurture the multitudes who are ready to hear God's word (9:12–13).

> *And taking the five loaves and the two fish, he looked up to heaven, and blessed and broke them, and gave them to the disciples to set before the crowd. And all ate and were filled. What was left over was gathered up, twelve baskets of broken pieces (9:16–17).*

This discipleship requires proper faith, namely faith resembling Jesus' openness to the power of God in his life, and faith regarding Jesus' true identity and mission. Some of his contemporaries thought that he was a reincarnation of John the Baptist, the prophet Elijah, or some other prophet. That is,

> *it was said by some that John had been raised from the dead, by some that Elijah had appeared, and by others that one of the ancient prophets had arisen (9:7–8).*

Indeed the Son of Man would himself, in Jesus' words, return from the dead.

> *The Son of Man must undergo great suffering, and be rejected by the elders, chief priests, and scribes, and be killed, and on the third day be raised' (9:22).*

To follow him on *this* path is to give up one's old life for the sake of a new and truer one. For, as he proclaimed to everyone,

> *'If any want to become my followers, let them deny themselves and take up their cross daily and follow me. For those who want to save their life will lose it, and those who lose their life for my sake will save it' (9:23–24).*

BREAKING BOUNDARIES

By the power of God the distance between death and life is so minimized that Jesus could be experienced by his disciples as one who conferred with certain persons who had died and who themselves could prophesy his death and resurrection.

> *While he was praying, the appearance of his face changed, and his clothes became dazzling white. Suddenly they saw two men, Moses and Elijah, talking to him. They appeared in glory and were speaking of his departure, which he was about to accomplish at Jerusalem. Now Peter and his companions were weighed down with sleep; but since they had stayed awake, they saw his glory and the two men who stood with him (9:29–32).*

Jesus' own powers, and such powers shared by his disciples, can be drawn upon by supposed outsiders, namely those who do not appear to disciples to be among his chosen associates. This is because of the alliance between all those whose helpful activities are not at odds with one another. For one day John remarked,

> *'Master, we saw someone casting out demons in your name, and we tried to stop him, because he does not follow with us.' But Jesus said to*

him, 'Do not stop him; for whoever is not against you is for you'
(9:49–50).

INTIMACY WITH GOD AND JESUS

With the powers that Jesus gives, disciples can not only exorcise and heal but are also immune from injury. Yet, Jesus cautioned, such privileges are not to be enjoyed as ends in themselves but as effects of the more important privilege of belonging to God.

> *'See, I have given you authority to tread on snakes and scorpions, and over all the power of the enemy; and nothing will hurt you. Nevertheless, do not rejoice at this, that the spirits submit to you, but rejoice that your names are written in heaven' (10:19–20).*

Jesus can give such powers because he has a special knowledge linked to an intimate association with God.

> *'All things have been handed over to me by my Father; and no one knows who the Son is except the Father, or who the Father is except the Son and anyone to whom the Son chooses to reveal him' (10:22).*

Relying on Jesus requires at least occasional intimacy with him, a closeness resulting in docility to his words. To Jesus a fine example of this was the attentive Mary, rather than her busy sister.

> *'Martha, Martha, you are worried and distracted by many things; there is need of only one thing. Mary has chosen the better part, which will not be taken away from her' (10:41–42).*

To be close to Jesus is to know the power of words to God. According to Jesus, God reacts to persistent requests like someone giving friends whatever they need (11:8).

> *'So I say to you, ask, and it will be given you; search, and you will find; knock, and the door will be opened for you' (11:9).*

At the same time however, and in line with the historians, prophets, and sages of Hebrew Scripture, Jesus cautions against

undue concern for wealth or material things. This, he says in parable, is like the rich hoarder whose life is taken in the night
(12:16–20). Jesus exhorts his disciples to radical trust in God.

> 'If God . . . clothes the grass of the field, which is alive today and
> tomorrow is thrown into the oven, how much more will he clothe you
> – you of little faith! And do not keep striving for what you are to eat
> and what you are to drink, and do not keep worrying. For it is the
> nations of the world that strive after all these things, and your Father
> knows that you need them. Instead, strive for his kingdom, and these
> things will be given to you as well' (12:28–31).

THE GOSPEL AND THE NEW AGE

As presented by Luke, Jesus' teachings — in word or by example
— largely accord with those of Hebrew Scripture. Jesus appears as
an astounding teacher, one who is dedicated to helping his people
understand the depth and spirit of their ancient and holy tradition.
He calls them to renewal in the faith of that tradition and to living
it with new depth and intensity. Having to this point compared the
New Age with teachings of Hebrew Scripture, we are prepared for
a similar comparison, namely between Jesus' teachings and those
of the New Age. Up to this point differences between the Bible
and the New Age have also been observed. In looking into the
Christian Scriptures, additional similarities and differences will
emerge in connection with teaching there that is not only by, but
also *about*, Jesus.

THE DIVINE AND THE HUMAN

According to Luke, Jesus' desire to be attuned to the word of God
and to trust it radically is rooted in the intimate relationship he
shares with God. In light of this relationship he speaks of God as
his Father, is honored by being called "Lord" and "Son of God,"
and is intimately associated with the presence of God.[3] After two of
his miracles — the raising of the young man and the expulsion of
the demons — the wondrous actions are immediately called

actions of God, in the first instance by onlookers (7:16) and in the second by Jesus himself (8:39). God's majesty is also recognized after Jesus rebukes an unclean spirit (9:43). Luke is bold and suggestive in this regard[4] even though such incidents, like Jesus' honorary titles and his references to God as Father, can be interpreted in different ways. In a traditional Jewish sense, Jesus could be understood as one like a prophet or king through whom God acts. In a later Christian sense Jesus' person and mission could be fully identified with the very presence and activity of God.

The New Age would present Jesus' awareness unambiguously as an example of human consciousness that is also divine. Christian tradition would say that as well, of course, without however extending the human-divine identity in this way to anyone other than Jesus. For many New Agers, Christ-consciousness involves intimacy with God, an association all persons can develop equally, be it Jesus or anyone else.[5] But in traditional Christianity only Jesus is regarded as both human and divine in a strict sense because only he is believed to be both by nature. The way a human-divine identity *is* believed to extend to others is discussed abstractly and at some length in the Pauline writings we will examine in the next chapter. At this point, however, some valuable perspectives on human closeness to God are apparent in Luke.

Jesus, says Luke, challenges disciples to grow in practical unanimity or oneness with God by exhibiting toward all others, even enemies, the kind of compassion and generosity that God is always ready to extend, even to the wicked. This is one of the most challenging ways in which the believer is commanded to be more like God. Such a command differs radically from the work of the serpent in Genesis who wanted the original man and woman to be "like God" by usurping God's authority as the ultimate arbiter of right and wrong (Gn 3:5). The way that Scripture then depicts humanity's oneness with God is quite nuanced and depends on a vision of goodness shared between the creator and the created.

The New Age view might be said to have fewer nuances because, by its monistic view of all reality, it regards human consciousness as essentially divine. Yet the New Age does distinguish between ego-centered faulty consciousness and self-centered, developed consciousness. The first is seen as incomplete and even harmful. As part of growth into the self, the second is thought to be healthy and desirable. This *self*-centeredness then appears more like human resemblance to God as the Bible presents it and thus more like one's life when saved in following Jesus (Lk 9:24). For both views — that of the New Age and that of the Bible — focus on greater identity with the divine. Both views involve "overtaking" God as Jacob did, namely by being self-assertive in the hands of God.

DIVINE FORGIVENESS

The parallel perceived here between the Bible and the New Age can be drawn even further by observing the importance of forgiveness in both perspectives. Jesus says in Luke that to be children of God the disciples must imitate God's mercy (6:35–36). In doing so they will exhibit something of God's very nature or character[6] since the totality of their love will mirror God's perfection.[7] Jesus' kind of compassion and forgiveness extends even to those who do not themselves show signs of overt repentance, as in the case of the paralytic to whom Jesus said,

> 'Stand up and take your bed and go to your home' (5:24).

To forgive, give, or lend expecting nothing in return is presented by Jesus as a part of what makes one more like God and thus in a position to live completely free from worry about sustenance or recompense.

In the New Age view, total forgiveness is highly regarded.[8] Like the generosity in almsgiving so highly praised in the Psalms and Sirach, generous and total forgiveness as seen by the New Age is a wondrous act of freedom, a miracle by which one is no longer held in bondage to the negative consciousness of grudges and vengefulness.[9] Rather one is free to influence one's world through the higher consciousness of creativity and love. In confronting problems and evils, not with judging but with compassion for even the evildoer, contamination by further evil is avoided, and a process of further contributing to the problem is halted.[10] By not condemning, one is left unbound. To be free like this is to be suited best for trusting the divine. In tune with the best of oneself, one is as close to the divine as may be possible.

This does not mean for Luke or the Bible as a whole that *God* demands no recompense for wrongdoing. Rather, the Lord holds persons firmly in account (11:51). In accord with Hebrew Scripture, John the Baptist teaches that God will punish all sins, even those of omission, from which one has finally refused to turn.

> *Even now the ax is lying at the root of the trees; every tree therefore that does not bear good fruit is cut down and thrown into the fire (3:9).*

Although it saddens him to see punitive measures taken against the unconverted (19:41, 44), Jesus teaches similarly (13:9), punishes certain evildoers himself (19:45), and attests clearly to the eventuality of divine justice, especially for those who know what God expects of them (12:48).

> *Nothing is covered up that will not be uncovered, and nothing secret that will not become known (12:2).*
>
> *That slave who knew what his master wanted, but did not prepare himself or do what was wanted, will receive a severe beating (12:47).*
>
> *There will be weeping and gnashing of teeth when you see Abraham and Isaac and Jacob and all the prophets in the kingdom of God, and you yourselves thrown out (13:28).*

While God may be characterized by vengefulness (21:22), Jesus cautions that this is one divine attribute, a prerogative, which the believer is *not* to imitate. Paul would likewise relate,

> *"Vengeance is mine, I will repay, says the LORD." (Rm 12:19).*

Therefore, as Luke recounts it, Jesus advises his disciples to shun prevailing modes of justice. Without denying the place of secular courts, he admonishes:

When you go with your accuser before a magistrate, on the way make an effort to settle the case, or you may be dragged before the judge, and the judge hand you over to the officer, and the officer throw you in prison (12:58).

The spirit of such a settlement should be such that the believer trusts that the things a person needs, including those demanded by justice, will be provided by God (12:28-30). Endowments by divine providence, along with resemblance to godliness itself, are thus aligned with the kind of forgiveness that never ceases (17:4).

HOLISTIC HARMONY

Other parallels to the New Age are perhaps easier to see. In Luke, Jesus says that by following him and thus belonging to God, the disciple is immune from harm. Jesus teaches this forthrightly without denying that following him also involves acceptance of the cross. The matter of suffering is a point with which, as we saw in connection with Sirach, the New Age seems to have some difficulty. More in accord with New Age perspective is Luke's reporting that Jesus' healing miracles are usually connected with the faith of the one healed. Associations like this between personal dispositions and effects in one's life display acceptance of a relationship we have already seen several times, namely that between authentic religiousness and bodily soundness. Here the biblical message continues to align with New Age views of holistic health where mental dispositions, including positive imagery, are thought to influence significantly bodily and spiritual well-being.[11]

According to the New Age the so-called right brain is engaged to help one move to higher consciousness with one's whole being, with one's heart and emotions, not just with one's intellect or through concepts. Imaging is thus regarded as critical in activating the will and passion that belong to all creativity and spiritual development.[12] A frequent methodology of New Age practice involves visualization or the use of guided imagery. Here an image is proposed for consideration or meditation so that through symbolism the one visualizing or imagining can grasp or become involved in something greater and more fulfilling.

We have observed how the Bible more often than not uses stories rather than abstract concepts to teach religious truths. A few examples typify the whole Bible. Truths about sin and redemption are presented wondrously through the creation accounts and ancestral narratives of Genesis. The Psalms constantly speak in imagery: a believer is like a tree planted by running water; God is like a shepherd. Jesus used the same technique when he spoke in parables: disobeying God is like the blind leading the blind; hearing God's word is like the ground's fruitful reception of seed; to hoard wealth is to be foolish like the rich man taken in the night. Jesus knew that vibrant faith often depends on lively images. The New Age, too, holds that it is often better not to spell things out fully but to use metaphors, symbols or stories so that understanding can be provoked through the listener's creative insight. Then those who have ears to hear can hear.[13] They can respond with heightened faith and perhaps be transformed.

PARANORMAL POWERS

At times however faith is not evident in one who is helped, as in the restoration of the dead to life, or in the case of the paralytic whom Jesus addresses and heals in light of others' faith.

> When he saw their faith, he said, 'Friend, your sins are forgiven you'
> (5:20).

Here perhaps we are allowed a glimpse into the unity of body, mind, and spirit where such unity transcends the individual. Jesus makes markedly apparent how one's positive thoughts, especially when conjoined with powerful words, can influence others and the environment.[14] Heightened consciousness can participate in the application of divine healing power.

Like Jesus, the disciples can heal and exorcise demons. By such deeds, Jesus and those who believe in him appear to have much in common with shamans, the folk healers who have captured New Age attention through their abilities to heal through the psychological and spiritual influence that their words bespeak.

In accord with the influence of consciousness on other reality, Simon can even, with faith in the suggestion of Jesus, catch fish. Without lessening the revelatory or spiritual implications of the catch as a sign of God's kingdom, the miracle can be seen as an example of psychokinesis[15] or the ability to move objects through mental or spiritual influence. In the literature of the New Age such abilities are linked with synchronicity whereby mind and all other reality relate in a way that goes beyond mere coincidence. Such occurrences appear to be more frequent in the lives of those who can calm the mind and enter deep states of meditation.[16]

It is important to note then that Jesus' work is quite dependent on the time he spends in prayer. Here we see that the work of God through an individual typically is conjoined with the awareness of God and God's will, a knowledge that such a person purposefully pursues. Such purposefulness relates to the persistence Jesus calls for in prayer. This, combined with faith often expressed in powerful words, relates to the New Age view whereby consciousness constitutes truth and affects external reality. Jesus taught that faith could move mountains (Mt 21:21); or as Luke tells it,

> 'If you had faith the size of a mustard seed, you could say to this mulberry tree, "Be uprooted and planted in the sea," and it would obey you' (17:6).

In face of the storm at sea Jesus' command to the wind and waves demonstrated such power. By asking the disciples in the boat, "Where is your faith?" he seems to imply that they could have left him to sleep and done the job as he did. Instead of accepting this about themselves, they marveled at the powers they saw in *him* (Lk 8:22–25).

Matthew says Jesus attributes great power to consensus or conscious agreement in bringing about a desired end.

> 'If two of you agree on earth about anything you ask, it will be done for you by my Father in heaven' (Mt 18:19).

For the New Age the unity that selves enjoy in their depth gives consensus enormous power to influence or effect external events.[17]

As Matthew depicts it, the power of consensus in prayer resides ultimately in Christ.

> *'For where two or three are gathered in my name, I am there among them' (Mt 18:20).*

In the gospels we see Jesus exercise such power every day. But he does not use his powers in a foolhardy way and thus succumb to temptations of Satan. Dispositions like those of Jesus, and like those who follow him and so resemble God in their own way, are part and parcel of the change of consciousness advocated in New Age philosophy: thought can be part of using higher powers, or at least powers not ordinarily drawn upon.

The ability to know other people's thoughts is a power that Luke frequently asserts Jesus had. Such ability depends on the paranormal powers of telepathy and clairvoyance.[18] These are not listed among those powers — such as preaching, nurturing, healing, and exorcising — that are transferred to the disciples whom Jesus regards as his kin. Yet Luke suggests that in practical terms there is very little difference between Jesus' ministry and the mission of his disciples.[19] Paranormal power that Jesus exhibits can thus be exhibited by others.

Luke had remarked early on how divination — in the form of casting lots — was used to choose Zechariah, the father of John the Baptist, as the officiating priest in the temple (1:9). In the Acts of the Apostles, the sequel to his gospel, Luke recounts how after Jesus' resurrection the disciples cast lots to name Matthias as one of the twelve apostles (Acts 1:26). Such divination was common and quite respected in the Greco-Roman or Hellenistic world of which the early church was a part.[20] Luke also mentions the presence of prophecy in the early Christian community (Acts 11:27; 13:1; 19:6) and connects it with faith and the gifts of the Spirit. The gift of prophecy is one of those most clearly associated with the paranormal powers respected by the New Age.

New Agers align themselves with researchers who point out that small children at about the age of four are increasingly found to have heightened paranormal powers. These abilities often go unrecognized, and children are apparently taught to disregard them in later years.[21] Jesus taught that becoming like a little child is essential to entering the kingdom of God (Lk 18:17). Perhaps Jesus sensed that childlike trust and openness bring with them paranormal powers he associated with discipleship.

LIFE AFTER DEATH

Also aligned with thought of the New Age may be the assumptions evident in the gospel that persons can return after dying. This is assumed to be possible with regard to Elijah and John the Baptist,[22] and Jesus claims that a return will be his own ultimate destiny. A reappearance like this might aptly be called a reincarnation, without however implying that the biblical intent is the same as the New Age one. In the latter view, one's return is part of a multiplicity of returns that are essential to salvation[23] or complete advancement into higher consciousness. For the Bible such reappearances are associated with a person's occasional return from a previous age or other condition. They are also associated with the fullness of glorified life that comes with resurrection. The biblical view of the matter appears to be captured in Hebrews 9:27:

> It is appointed for mortals to die once, and after that the judgment. . . .

Yet the thin line between the living and the dead, so evident to New Agers for whom spiritualism or other contact with the dead is commonplace, becomes apparent when the transfigured Jesus confers with Moses and Elijah. During the time of David in ancient Israel, Saul conferred with the deceased Samuel in a manner that was expressly spiritualistic.

> Saul said to his servants, 'Seek out for me a woman who is a medium, so that I may go to her and inquire of her.' . . . They came to the woman by night. And he said, 'Consult a spirit for me, and bring up for me the one whom I name to you.' . . . The woman said, 'Whom shall I bring up for you?' He answered, 'Bring up Samuel for me.' Then Samuel said to Saul, 'Why have you disturbed me by bringing me up?' Saul answered, 'I am in great distress, for the Philistines are warring

> *against me, and God has turned away from me and answers me no*
> *more, either by prophets or by dreams; so I have summoned you to tell*
> *me what I should do.' Samuel said, . . . 'Because you did not obey the*
> *voice of the LORD, and did not carry out his fierce wrath against*
> *Amalek, therefore the LORD has done this thing to you today.'*
> *Immediately Saul fell full length on the ground, filled with fear*
> *because of the words of Samuel. . . . (1 Sm 28:7–8, 11, 15–16, 18, 20).*

There is no hint in the story that Samuel was not real or that his message was not from God. Even though many of Saul's divinatory practices had not worked, apparently because of God's reticence to approach him in this way, Samuel is allowed to appear in order to bring the bad news of Saul's impending doom. Although the upshot of the vision is negative, it parallels God's own appearances years earlier to the youthful Samuel.[24] Such contact demonstrated to Israel that Samuel was "a trustworthy prophet of the LORD" (I Sm 3:20).

Clearly, Luke does not want to suggest that the presence of Moses and Elijah was bogus, but that they had come from beyond and were helpful in both establishing Jesus' identity and confirming his mission.[25] The shortsighted Peter however could not see this.

> *Peter said to Jesus, 'Master, it is good for us to be here; let us make three*
> *dwellings, one for you, one for Moses, and one for Elijah' — not know-*
> *ing what he said (9:33).*

He was however welcoming and hospitable. Luke reports a similar kind of shortsightedness in connection with the appearance of the dead and risen Jesus to the disciples on the road to Emmaus. They talked with him and welcomed him into their home but did not understand the significance of his presence and words until

> *he had been made known to them in the breaking of the bread (24:35).*

With greater consciousness of the implications, Christians in other settings would profess to have conferred with and welcomed the dead when they experienced the newly risen Christ or, in much later ages, rejoiced at his appearances, those of his mother, Mary, or those of other saints. Such interaction with persons who have passed from this life has doubtlessly, though not always with solemn approbation of church leaders, been regarded as acceptable because it appears to be part of God's plan or, as Ben Sira put it, "sent by intervention from the Most High" (Sir 34:6). Deuteronomy's injunctions against consulting spirits and ghosts are not believed to apply in such cases. Even outside the contexts of biblical faith, those who consult the dead know the importance of distinguishing wise and reliable spirits from troubled and malicious ones.[26] So apparitions of benevolent spirits, for healing or advice, are often more welcomed by New Agers than by many modern Christians, which can show how difficult it is at times to judge who clearly belongs to what group.

INSIDERS AND OUTSIDERS

Luke's gospel is manifestly designed to facilitate universal Christian faith, to encourage faith in Jesus Christ through acceptance of a gospel "proclaimed in his name to all nations" (24:47). Yet, according to Luke's portrayal, Jesus also displays flexibility in assigning persons to categories, as he did with regard to those who, though not with him and his disciples, were casting out demons in his name (9:49–50). Jesus' tolerant attitude toward those not of the inner circle may also connote respect for them.[27] Shortly after the incident a Samaritan village refused to welcome him.

> When his disciples James and John saw it, they said, 'LORD, do you want us to command fire to come down from heaven and consume them?' But he turned and rebuked them. Then they went on to another village (9:54–56).

Moreover, Jesus' strong cautions against judging others warn us that even the most faithful are in danger of drawing too hasty conclusions about the fate of their neighbors. For the New Age, judgment is a hindrance to personal growth and consciousness because it can set illusory barriers between persons and build needless differences that can work contrary to the unity of all.[28] This is not to say that we have found complete agreement between the New Age and the Bible respecting their acceptance of one another, or respecting the various religions and other possible paths to God. It does suggest that among the approaches to consciousness and godliness there is more room for agreement than may at first be evident.

Notes

1. Fitzmyer, *Luke (I–IX)*, 9–10, 20, 57.
2. For example: Frederick W. Danker, *Jesus and the New Age: A Commentary on St. Luke's Gospel* (Philadelphia: Fortress, 1988), 9–13.
3. Fitzmyer, *Luke (I–IX)*, 193, 202–3, 207–8, 218–19.
4. Fitzmyer, *Luke (I–IX)*, 740, 810.
5. John White, "Enlightenment and the Christian Tradition" in *What Is Enlightenment?*, ed. John White (Los Angeles: Tarcher, 1984), 126–27.
6. David Gooding, *According to Luke: A New Exposition of the Third Gospel* (Grand Rapids, MI: Eerdmans, 1987), 121.
7. I. Howard Marshall, *The Gospel of Luke: A Commentary on the Greek Text* (Grand Rapids, MI: Eerdmans, 1978), 265.
8. Zukav, *Seat of the Soul*, 226–228.
9. *Course in Miracles*, 246–48.
10. Zukav, *Seat of the Soul*, 72.
11. Capra, *Uncommon Wisdom*, 153.
12. Pearce, *Magical Child Matures*, 121–23.
13. Capra, *Uncommon Wisdom*, 75–78.
14. Heaney, *Sacred and the Psychic*, 68.
15. Heaney, *Sacred and the Psychic*, 42.
16. Peter Russell, *The Global Brain: Speculations on the Evolutionary Leap to Planetary Consciousness* (Los Angeles: Tarcher, 1983), 212–19.
17. Roberts, *Individual and Mass Events*, 104, 110, 114–31.
18. Heaney, *Sacred and the Psychic*, 22.
19. O. C. Edwards, Jr., *Luke's Story of Jesus* (Philadelphia: Fortress, 1981), 50.
20. Richard I. Pervo, *Profit with Delight: The Literary Genre of the Acts of the Apostles* (Philadelphia: Fortress, 1987), 39–40.
21. Joseph Chilton Pearce, *Magical Child: Rediscovering Nature's Plan for Our Children* (New York: Dutton, 1977), 127–37.
22. Barbara Clow, "Reincarnation as Method for the Divine Quest" *in Fireball and the Lotus*, ed. Ron Miller and Jim Kenney (Santa Fe, NM: Bear, 1987), 236.

23. Heaney, *Sacred and the Psychic*, 213–14.

24. Robert Polzin, *Samuel and the Deuteronomist: A Literary Study of the Deuternomonic History. Part Two. I Samuel* (San Francisco: Harper, 1989), 219–20.

25. Marshall, *The Gospel of Luke*, 384–85.

26. Villoldo and Krippner, *Healing States*, 15–16.

27. Fitzmyer, *Luke (I–IX)*, 820.

28. Spangler, *Revelation*, 170, 178.

CHAPTER 7

The Glory of the Lord

Philippians 1–4; Colossians 1–4; Ephesians 1–4

GOD AND THE TRUE SELF

P aul of Tarsus, Christianity's great missionary during the apostolic age, encountered resistance to his message and suffered at the hands of both civil and religious authorities. His Epistle to the Philippians was written from prison to Christians who were confused by teachings differing from his and who were troubled by disputes and bickering among themselves. The consistent source of Paul's message is, despite his imprisonment, his joy in the Lord or Christ.

The epistle appears to some scholars as a composite of three separate letters or parts of letters.[1] In what is claimed by some to be an older section, Paul affirms that he can cope with any circumstance because of a valuable disposition:

> *I have learned to be content with whatever I have. (4:11b).*

This kind of self-sufficiency is no enslaving self-centeredness but a freeing kind of dependence on the Lord.

> *I can do all things through him who strengthens me. (4:13).*

For the Lord is bounteous and quite dependable. God manifests

> *his riches in glory in Christ Jesus (4:19)*

and out of them provides anything that is needed.

The generous sustenance of God extends beyond needs to actions or responsibilities that are part of a believer's full and rewarding life.

> *I am confident of this, that the one who began a good work among you will bring it to completion by the day of Jesus Christ (1:6).*

So Paul prays that his readers may profit from God's generous blessing in both consciousness and experience.

> *And this is my prayer, that your love may overflow more and more with knowledge and full insight (1:9).*

MAKING THE MOST OF DIFFERENCES

Already in the church there were disputing factions. Some were motivated by unfriendly competition with Paul.

> *Some proclaim Christ from envy and rivalry, but others from goodwill (1:15).*

Some were intriguing against him. They

> *proclaim Christ out of selfish ambition, not sincerely but intending to increase my suffering in my imprisonment (1:17).*

Apparently they desired to silence him. But Paul can see good in all of this. For in every case the gospel is at least being preached, and that is a source of joy.

> *What does it matter? Just this, that Christ is proclaimed in every way, whether out of false motives or true; and in that I rejoice. Yes, and I will continue to rejoice (1:18).*

Like Ben Sira and Jesus, Paul recommends dispositions like these instead of negative ones.

> *Rejoice in the LORD always; again I will say, Rejoice. Let your gentleness be known to everyone. The LORD is near. Do not worry about anything, but in everything by prayer and supplication with thanksgiving let your requests be made known to God. And the peace of God, which surpasses all understanding, will guard your hearts and your minds in Christ Jesus (4:4–7).*

Paul does not need to worry about disputes between different groups or factions. He can look beyond factionalism to the bigger picture. The contentiousness or arguing will, in Paul's mind, even work to the good.

> *It is my eager expectation and hope that I will not be put to shame in any way, but that by my speaking with all boldness, Christ will be exalted now as always in my body, whether by life or by death (1:20).*

THE BASIS OF TRUE HUMILITY

Indeed Paul is convinced of the ultimate rightness of the gospel. One struggles at times for it but is rewarded by salvation.

> *And this is God's doing (1:28b).*

> *More than that, I regard everything as loss because of the surpassing value of knowing Christ Jesus my LORD. For his sake I have suffered the loss of all things, and I regard them as rubbish, in order that I may gain Christ and be found in him, not having a righteousness of my own that comes from the law, but one that comes through faith in Christ, the righteousness from God based on faith (3:8–9).*

So the enthusiasm that various Christians have for their own messages is understandable. Nonetheless, Christians' rivalries and conceits should be replaced by humility and even by service of those whose views are opposed.

> *If then there is any encouragement in Christ, any consolation from love, any sharing in the Spirit, any compassion and sympathy, make my joy complete: be of the same mind, having the same love, being in full accord and of one mind. Do nothing from selfish ambition or conceit, but in humility regard others as better than yourselves. Let each of you look not to your own interests, but to the interests of others. Do all things without murmuring and arguing, so that you may be blameless and innocent, children of God without blemish in the midst of a crooked and perverse generation, in which you shine like stars in the world (2:1–4, 14–15).*

For this, Christ was a prime example, in his birth and in his death,

> *who, though he was in the form of God,*
> *did not regard equality with God*
> *as something to be exploited,*
> *but emptied himself,*
> *taking the form of a slave,*
> *being born in human likeness.*
> *And being found in human form,*
> *he humbled himself*
> *and became obedient to the point of death —*
> *even death on a cross.*
> *Therefore God also highly exalted him*
> *and gave him the name*
> *that is above every name,*
> *so that at the name of Jesus*
> *every knee should bend,*
> *in heaven and on earth and under the earth,*
> *and every tongue should confess*
> *that Jesus Christ is* Lord,
> *to the glory of God the Father (2:6–11).*

The Basis of True Maturity

Christians so humble can thus live in joyful hope of an exaltation similar to the risen Christ's. In such faith they can

know Christ and the power of his resurrection and the sharing of his
sufferings by becoming like him in his death (3:10).

The process of conforming to Christ is never complete in this life, and no Christian is exempt from the process no matter how mature or informed in the faith one may be.

Beloved, I do not consider that I have made it my own; but this one
thing I do: forgetting what lies behind and straining forward to what
lies ahead, I press on toward the goal for the prize of the heavenly call
of God in Christ Jesus. Let those of us then who are mature be of the
same mind (3:13–15a).

WISDOM AND BEHAVIOR

The author of the Epistle to the Colossians is clearly in the Pauline tradition but, according to modern historical criticism, not literally Paul himself.[2] The author develops established Pauline themes creatively and uses words in a unique style. For convenience or by way of conviction the author may be called "Paul" in the traditional manner. Of particular concern in his letter are dispositions he associated with those committed to Christ.

Paul prays that his readers may grow in their faith through wisdom and knowledge. These he sees in a reciprocal relationship with virtuous behavior. This means that, like Sirach who understood how speech and actions influence one another, Paul recommends heightened consciousness as a counterpart of increasingly desirable deeds. It is all part of advancing in knowledge of "the grace of God" (1:6), namely in awareness of that saving love of God that, in Pauline terms, is poured into the hearts of believers through Christ and the Holy Spirit (Rom 5:1–5).

We have not ceased praying for you and asking that you may be filled
with the knowledge of God's will in all spiritual wisdom and under-
standing, so that you may lead lives worthy of the LORD, fully pleasing
to him, as you bear fruit in every good work and as you grow in the
knowledge of God (1:9–10).

LIKENESS TO GOD

Such a life is one of redemption from sin and ignorance; it is acceptance by God who loves like a parent taking children into the light-filled domain of Christ (1:12).

> He has rescued us from the power of darkness and transferred us into the kingdom of his beloved Son, in whom we have redemption, the forgiveness of sins (1:13–14).

Though with far less emphasis than Luke,[3] Paul sees forgiveness as one of the primary characteristics of God (see also 3:13 and Eph 1:7; 4:32). Thus he emphasizes the universality (Rom 4:9–12) of Psalm 32:1–2, which he cites:

> 'Blessed are those whose iniquities are forgiven,
>   and whose sins are covered;
> blessed is the one against whom the Lord will not reckon
>   sin' (Rom 4:7–8).

This is part of Paul's theological anthropology, his view of human nature insofar as it has been drawn into the life of God through faith and is manifest through virtuous living.

Paul's alignment of redemption with faith-filled knowledge of God harmonizes with the biblical visions of humanity and wholeness we have seen so far. By these views the fullness of human life appears as participation or cooperation in elements of divine life. Human life is seen in Genesis and Psalms as sharing in God's own power to produce life and to take charge of nature and the environment. In Sirach the blessed person partakes of God's own wisdom and is a source of quite influential speech. For Luke disciples are like children resembling their divine parent because they exhibit characteristics of God, especially by forgiving wrongs done to them. Attention to the power of speech allows the miracles of Jesus and the disciples to be compared with the power of God's creative word. Relevant texts are worth recalling:

> God created humankind in his image, in the image of God he created
> them; male and female he created them. God blessed them, and God

*said to them, 'Be fruitful and multiply, and fill the earth and subdue
it; and have dominion over the fish of the sea and over the birds of the
air and over every living thing that moves upon the earth' (Gn
1:27–28).*

*What are human beings that you are mindful of them, mortals that
you care for them? Yet you have made them a little lower than God,
and crowned them with glory and honor. You have given them dominion over the works of your hands; you have put all things under their
feet (Ps 8:4–6).*

*The Lord created human beings out of the earth. . . .
He endowed them with strength like his own
        and made them in his own image . . .
            and gave them dominion over beasts and birds.
Discretion and tongue . . . he gave them (Sir 17:1a, 3, 4b, 6).*

*'Love your enemies, do good, and lend, expecting nothing in return.
Your reward will be great, and you will be children of the Most High;
for he is kind to the ungrateful and the wicked. Be merciful, just as
your Father is merciful' (Lk 6:35–36).*

Paul develops insights like these by focusing on the Christian's
life as participation in Christ's life. Such sharing is a gift or grace
that comes with faith and the divine presence of the Holy Spirit.
Forgiven and dwelling in intimacy with Christ, the believer enjoys
closeness to God. Paul uses some technical terms to depict the specialness of the redeemer. As the "image" of God (see below as well
as 2 Cor 4:4), Christ mirrors the divine essence in a way that far
exceeds the resemblance of humans generally or believers in particular. According to Genesis, Psalms, Sirach, and Luke, such
resemblance leaves humans generally subordinate to God. Though
godly by blessing and by participation in divine life, they are
ungodly in comparison with the fullness of divine being.

New Likeness to God

For Paul, however, Christ is the "firstborn of all creation"; he is
the one in whom divine power operates, first in having created the
universe and, second, in continuing to maintain order in all things.

Here is a cosmic vision of the whole Christ.[4] His overall presence and primacy acquire additionally a new dimension in his becoming the "first-born of the dead."[5] For by his cross and resurrection, Christ brought *new* life to the world and *intensified divine intimacy* with the world. It is in this new intimacy as redeeming reconciliation with God (1:14) that believers live by faith and fullness of grace. This union, says Paul, makes them members of Christ's risen body, members of the church.

> He is the image of the invisible God, the firstborn of all creation; for in him all things in heaven and on earth were created, things visible and invisible, whether thrones or dominions or rulers or powers – all things have been created through him and for him. He himself is before all things, and in him all things hold together. He is the head of the body, the church; he is the beginning, the firstborn from the dead, so that he might come to have first place in everything. For in him all the fullness of God was pleased to dwell, and through him God was pleased to reconcile to himself all things, whether on earth or in heaven, by making peace through the blood of his cross (1:15–20).

All of this participation in the divine mystery is connected with a knowledge or consciousness by which the believer can move forward to final glory. By God's word all of this becomes proclaimed as

> the mystery that has been hidden throughout the ages and generations but has now been revealed to his saints. To them God chose to make known how great among the Gentiles are the riches of the glory of this mystery, which is Christ in you, the hope of glory ... [,] all the riches of assured understanding, and ... the knowledge of God's mystery, that is, Christ himself, in whom are hidden all the treasures of wisdom and knowledge (1:26–27; 2:2–3).

UNFINISHED KNOWLEDGE AND RENEWAL IN LIFE

This is thus a knowledge that must grow to fullness, resisting any alien philosophies based on principles opposed to Christ. Like Ben Sira who repudiates paranormal powers not from God, Paul warns against visions not rooted in Christ (2:18), but also against harmful ways of understanding. Such an admonition is paralleled in the account of Paul's exorcising the troublesome fortune-teller (Acts 16:16–18). Christ is the focus. So Christians should be

> rooted and built up in him and established in the faith, just as you were taught, abounding in thanksgiving. See to it that no one takes you captive through philosophy and empty deceit, according to human tradition, according to the elemental spirits of the universe, and not according to Christ. For in him the whole fullness of deity dwells bodily, and you have come to fullness in him . . . (2:7–10).

The believer's relationship to Christ is made visible in baptism, the ritual of death and new life. The Christian is thus presented as one who is reborn, or reincarnated, not literally as delivery from the womb or entry into a new body, but really insofar as a spiritual resurrection or transformation takes place.

> When you were buried with him in baptism, you were also raised with him through faith in the power of God, who raised him from the dead (2:12).

The Christian is thus part of a process of resurrection and growth as a member of Christ's body:

> The substance belongs to Christ . . . from whom the whole body, nourished and held together by its ligaments and sinews, grows with a growth that is from God. For you have died, and your life is hidden with Christ in God. When Christ who is your life is revealed, then you also will be revealed with him in glory (2:17, 19; 3:3–4).

In the specialness of this relationship Christians are called to great responsibility and joyous devotion, to mirroring the life of God in themselves.

> So if you have been raised with Christ, seek the things that are above, where Christ is, seated at the right hand of God. As God's chosen ones, holy and beloved, clothe yourselves with compassion, kindness, humility, meekness, and patience. Bear with one another and, if anyone has

> *a complaint against another, forgive each other; just as the* Lord *has forgiven you, so you also must forgive. Above all, clothe yourselves with love, which binds everything together in perfect harmony. And let the peace of Christ rule in your hearts, to which indeed you were called in the one body. And be thankful. Let the word of Christ dwell in you richly; teach and admonish one another in all wisdom; and with gratitude in your hearts sing psalms, hymns, and spiritual songs to God (3:1, 12–16).*

Such a life must be nurtured by regular and purposeful communications with God.

> *Devote yourselves to prayer, keeping alert in it with thanksgiving (4:2).*

Relating to Outsiders

Though forming a special group, Christians should deal kindly with anyone who is not visibly part of their household of faith. Their interaction with the outside should be flavored by the consciousness and behavior appropriate to Christ.

> *Conduct yourselves wisely toward outsiders, making the most of the time. Let your speech always be gracious, seasoned with salt, so that you may know how you ought to answer everyone. (4:5–6).*

Enlightened Consciousness

Like Colossians, the Epistle to the Ephesians is written in the spirit of the Pauline tradition. In many ways the letter is a summary of Paul's teachings but does not appear to much modern historical criticism to have come directly from the named author.[6]

"Paul" opens with praise to God whose intimacy with the believer is complete through Christ, a closeness endowed with all heavenly riches and imparting honorable status akin to Christ's (1:3–14). The perspective on the relationship of the Christian to God is similar to Colossians'. Christians not averting to this wondrous relationship need prayer that their insight may be deepened and their consciousness raised to knowing their identity and power, characteristics of God's holy ones, which resemble Christ's. Paul prays that they may receive

> *a spirit of wisdom and revelation as you come to know him, so that, with the eyes of your heart enlightened, you may know what is the hope to which he has called you . . . and what is the immeasurable greatness of his power for us who believe, according to the working of his great power. God put this power to work in Christ when he raised him from the dead and seated him at his right hand in the heavenly places (1:17–20).*

And they should also remember that out of great love, God

> *raised us up with him and seated us with him in the heavenly places in Christ Jesus (2:6).*

Indeed it is the fullness of God in Christ that fills the church and the universe. For God

> *has put all things under his feet and has made him the head over all things for the church, which is his body, the fullness of him who fills all in all. (1:22–23).*

THE GRACE OF GOD

Christians' heavenly inheritance is thus neither due to them nor merely earned by them. Rather it is the result of God's pure love and favor. The essence of the project is divine.

> *For by grace you have been saved through faith, and this is not your own doing; it is the gift of God — not the result of works, so that no one may boast. (2:8–9).*

Like a building becoming increasingly a dwelling place of the divine, the church has a capstone in Christ.

> *In him the whole structure is joined together and grows into a holy temple in the LORD; in whom you also are built together spiritually into a dwelling place for God (2:21–22).*

Such intimacy with God is the basis of a lively trust. In Christ

> *we have access to God in boldness and confidence through faith in*
> *him. (3:12).*

Christians enjoy then a new experiential identity with God in all God's fullness, a loving identity of both consciousness and action, a closeness that surpasses imagining. Paul prays that

> *you may have the power to comprehend, with all the saints, what is*
> *the breadth and length and height and depth, and to know the love of*
> *Christ that surpasses knowledge, so that you may be filled with all the*
> *fullness of God. Now to him who by the power at work within us is*
> *able to accomplish abundantly far more than all we can ask or imag-*
> *ine, to him be glory . . . (3:18–21).*

Such knowledge and behavior need constant renewal. Christians must grow beyond the consciousness of unenlightened minds; along with this they must overcome callousness and licentiousness (4:18–19). Their state must be one of ever higher consciousness and ever holier living.

> *You were taught to put away your former way of life, your old self, cor-*
> *rupt and deluded by its lusts, and to be renewed in the spirit of your*
> *minds, and to clothe yourselves with the new self, created according to*
> *the likeness of God in true righteousness and holiness (4:22–24).*

POSITIVE THOUGHT

Comparing the Pauline literature with the interests of the New Age yields much for consideration. Immediately apparent is the great power of Paul's positive disposition. These are the kinds of attitudes that the New Age sees as essential to overcoming faulty consciousness and attaining happiness. Through a change of disposition, says the New Age, one can let go of dreariness and fear of all sorts. One can learn to abide in permanent peace by being attentive to God who is present both powerfully and faithfully.[7] In such peace, gratitude can be quite energizing and demonstrate great healing power.[8] Gratitude allows even common experience to be appreciated with new wonder and vitality.[9]

Even when writing from prison, Paul can give thanks for blessings received and focus on the valuable possibilities in the situations he is facing. His joy is centered on God.[10] He suffers indeed but does not let himself be lowered into the defeating morass of self-pity and animosity. He thus can be open by his faith to the fuller power and protection of God in his life,[11] a fullness he wishes for all who read him, and a fullness that he is confident is theirs by God's grace.

If they would only act upon this their lives would be changed; they would continue to be transformed for the heavenly bliss that awaits them. This is "self-sufficiency" that depends first and foremost on the generosity of God.[12] It thus relates to Ben Sira's conviction that saying this or that would be better for me is frequently useless. It is also links with the optimism of the Psalmist who professes, in light of the Lord's shepherding, to be permanently provided with all that is really needed. So Paul stresses the importance of continued enriching communication with God through prayer.[13] To express bodily one's spiritual union with God, and to reinforce one's growing disposition toward it, the believer should rejoice, be bold in speech, and sing aloud in hymns of praise.

GROWTH IN NEW LIFE

The New Age themes touching on the divinity of human consciousness and on the body-mind-spirit unity have much in common with such Pauline dispositions. They attest what Paul has found to be true: that how we think is intertwined with how we act.[14] And how we think and act can, with confidence in God, with a trust born of thanksgiving, be part of a blissful and godly presence in the world. This presence is for Paul part of an ongoing process of growth in truth, of straining resolutely toward his goal, of emergence into ever greater solidarity with God in the present life through increasing participation in heavenly life by union with Christ. In this respect the believer can always wonder about the sufficiency of any level of maturity achieved.[15]

The New Age accepts the view of contemporary science that our understanding of reality is always in progress, always improving mere approximations of the truth we are seeking.[16] Within the Pauline view of things, one cannot in this life make too much progress, no matter how mature one becomes or how much consciousness one achieves. Paul stresses this over and over again. There always remains before one a higher state of life and a higher state of consciousness. One's old life must increasingly give way to the new.[17] In New Age perspective one grows spiritually by constantly relinquishing a limited intellectual grasp of the divine will to which one is surrendering.[18]

Surely for Paul such advancement — the desired consequence of a new life begun with faith and baptism — is sustained by grace and the Holy Spirit. It is part of life in Christ, and Paul describes its earthly form in terms of a single lifetime. It is not, as for the New Age, an emergence into one's natural divinity that progresses in a single lifetime and then, through subsequent reincarnations, continues to develop in later earthly lifetimes.

In both cases, however, higher consciousness is an integral part of advancement toward the goal of unity with the divine. Paul does rely on belief in rebirth, which is a reincarnation in a certain sense. Entry into the Christian life, he says, is a dying and rising into a new earthly life with a heavenly inheritance; it is being saved by grace, being born again through death and resurrection into Christ. It is an ever-greater likeness to God because of divine forgiveness[19] that the Bible, from Genesis on, teaches is continuous. This new life is the basis of hope in another new form of life after death, of hope in resurrection into the glory of heaven, when Christ appears again at the end of this age. Confidence in such new life is perhaps the closest the Bible can come to anything like the New Age conviction regarding reincarnation.

THE ONENESS OF ALL

Related to this view of ongoing life is the Pauline and New Age sense of the unity of humanity and the universe. Contemporary physics and physiology theorize that because of the interpenetrating character of all reality at a deep level, humanity and all of nature may enjoy an organismic or living unity.[20] Utilizing concepts borrowed at least in part from Hellenistic or Greek philosophy,[21] Paul sees this unity as a common sharing in the work of Christ as the "firstborn of creation"; through him the whole universe, with everyone in it, is held providentially in the hands of God; through him the cosmos or universe enjoys unity in God.

This work is manifest and intensified through Jesus' resurrection because of which, by God's favor or grace, all believers become the Body of Christ. Christ thus has a unifying character on a cosmic scale.[22] Here divine grace attains universal proportions. Paul remains essentially consistent with his vision of human *participation* in the divine, though Ephesians 1:22–23 may come closer to monism — and thus to the New Age view that everything *is* divine — than any other place in the Christian Scripture. God in Christ

> *put all things beneath his feet and gave him as head over all things to the church, which is his body, the fullness of the one who fills all things in every way.*

Not clear here is the way *all* is *one* since it is not easy to see what distinction is being made between Christ, the church, and the cosmos as the divine fullness is said to be poured forth.[23] The text seems to allow for a certain reciprocity to be found between God, Christ, the church, and all creation. Such a view, like Ben Sira's notion of God as all in all, could be understood in a monistic way.[24] But to come close to monism, or to seeing all things as essentially divine, is not the same as replicating monism. Overall Paul, like Ben Sira, remains firm in his view of creation, humanity, and the church as participants in varying degrees in the life of God and Christ. Here there is both unity and distinction, unity with God and difference from God.

The New Age sees the divine-human togetherness as a solidarity of all in the divine life, in the oneness of being that is the greatest truth. Life is part of an organized system where something like a mind holds all things in unity.[25] It is important to observe that the New Age's unifying or holistic vision of reality is not designed to dethrone God but to retrieve a vision that has in many ways been lost with the rise of modern sciences. In a unifying view of reality where consciousness is part of nature, one can find anew a certain charm and dignity in all things. One can also see their relatedness and thus marvel anew at both nature and humanity.[26]

Nonetheless the New Age does claim that there may be no essential difference between divinity and the true self, only between divinity and the selfish or unenlightened ego.[27] The Christ as the New Age understands him, the universal essence of all life, serves as a source and goal by nurturing all persons and by drawing them ever higher into fuller being and bliss.[28] Again, however, Paul's view of faith-filled human nature relates to this. For he states repeatedly in various ways how the Christian must always be putting aside the old life in favor of a new self that has a mind renewed by the Spirit of God. This relates directly to the conversion, the change of mind and heart, for which Jesus calls. Change of this kind means moving from sinful or ego-centered existence to a mode of higher consciousness where one becomes ever more centered on God.[29]

In either case, that of Paul or the New Age, the well-being of individuals is understood as interrelated, so that the pain of one, being the pain of all, can be overcome by a joyful concern to serve those in need. Pain is always shared pain, consciously or unconsciously. Paul does not explicitly include, as does the New Age, the pain of a suffering environment. His vision of the cosmic Christ, the Christ who is the "firstborn of creation," does however allow for it. In him all creation is seen theologically or religiously as unified by the providential and redemptive design of God.

Among the ecologists of the New Age, the earth is viewed as suffering when the inherent harmony of the complexly intertwining systems of life is aggressively perturbed.[30] But in such aggression the individual suffers too. For the full self far transcends the single ego and holds the individual into unity with all dimensions of nature and spirit.[31] So for Paul and the New Age, happiness is always shared happiness, redounding to the blessedness or health of all creatures and all creation. Paul sees that God, living in all things, bears them together into the fullness of their being, transforming them by divine power and grace.[32] Heightened self-consciousness and greater self-sufficiency thus go hand in hand with heightened God-consciousness and greater solidarity with all one's brothers and sisters and with one's whole environment. On this Paul and the New Age can be said to see eye to eye.

RESPECTFUL DIALOGUE

Paul's exhortations to deal kindly with the factions that opposed him recommend much change for dispositions that sometimes separate Christians from New Agers. Acceptance is the key, along with remembering that even those who do not teach what one sees as fully true can contribute to spreading at least part of the truth in which one believes. Indeed in Philippians Paul is thinking of differing *Christian* factions who, in his view, should deal with one another humbly.[33] Even as they look to Christ for manifestations of godly qualities, so should they look for the grace of God working in others.[34]

But in Colossians, it is simply "outsiders," non-Christians,[35] who are mentioned. A cosmic vision, such as Paul's perspective on Christ as firstborn of creation and as the redeeming risen head of the church, allows for ecumenism of a very deep sort; it allows for a radical acceptance of the divine goodness or grace that unites all people, even those of varying cultures and religious traditions. Such a vision can be the best foundation for peace of all sorts, even on a global scale.[36] Paul's cosmic vision would appear then to allow for a sense of some solidarity — though hardly complete agreement — between a biblical view of redeemed creation and the New Age principles related to the oneness of all and to the validity of various paths toward divinity.

It may be more appropriate however to extend Paul's suggestions to differences between those of biblical faith and those of New Age persuasion. Surely the two groups do not agree on many things. But, having found what they have in common, they can serve their own interests by serving one another's needs. First of all it should be noted that many Jews and Christians accept certain New Age principles. Yet there appear to be New Age teachings that are remarkably different from those of the Bible. Indeed Paul warns against alien teachings and beliefs while pointing out their incongruity with faith as he knows it. But as the sapiential and other biblical writers do, he also adapts such teachings to his own purposes.

In light of biblical material we have examined, we can see his caution and finesse as part of what one might expect from a religion's central scripture, namely firmness in promoting a particular kind of faith and no other. For Paul, the knowledge that comes with loving Christ is the supreme kind of knowledge[37] that takes precedence over any other philosophy or form of consciousness. But other philosophies or forms of consciousness can, as his writings attest, be brought into service of the Christ-consciousness he promoted.

According to the New Age, resistance to the views or influence of a real or supposed adversary breeds needless pain and sorrow when it does not flow from heightened consciousness.[38] There is much more to be gained by focusing first on possible agreement. The New Age listens carefully to contemporary scientists whose visions include the implicate order, the deeper stratum in which all reality is enfolded. One's sense of this order, they say, is typically connected with specific ideas about life and truth, or at least with tacit assumptions in that regard. Such ideas and assumptions can become rigid and nonnegotiable and thus be defended vehemently, even violently. This is especially true when one's sense of the implicate order involves the notions and customs of areas in science, politics, or religion that powerfully influence individuals and cultures.

Movement toward greater truth and toward a heightened sense of the totality in which all is unified brings with it a new sense of order. Sense attained in this way thus requires both a deepened notion of self and a willingness to suspend judgment about the absolute nature of one's ideas and assumptions. Suspension of this kind can take place in a dialogue where one attempts to hold various views at once with the aim of approaching and expressing truth in a fresh and creative way. In short, it means listening to one another with open-mindedness and respect.[39] The experience of universal unity and love, says the New Age, depends on looking for points of agreement rather than points of separation.[40]

It is easier to take Paul's advice, to regard others as more important than oneself, if one remembers one's own deficiencies.

Followers of the Bible and the New Age need not ignore this. Both groups assume or make an act of faith in the divine power that surpasses all evil. Surely the two groups can learn from one another.[41] But they can go even further, boldly perhaps in face of unfounded criticism and despite unfounded fear. By affirming one another in their mutually perceived good, by propagating one another's mutually perceived truths, both groups can have the greatest confidence that whatever errors or evil lurk in either one will eventually be outdone. And for that, according to the principles of each group, more power must be attributed to the divine than to the judgments and machinations of sinful or ego-centered humans.

Notes

1. F. F. Bruce, *Philippians: A Good News Commentary* (San Francisco: Harper, 1983), *xxvi–xviii*.

2. J. L. Houlden, *Paul's Letters from Prison: Philippians, Colossians, Philemon, and Ephesians* (Philadelphia: Westminster, 1970), 134–39.

3. Houlden, *Paul's Letters*, 155.

4. Fox, *Cosmic Christ*, 90–91.

5. Houlden, *Paul's Letters*, 170–71.

6. Houlden, *Paul's Letters*, 235–37, 251–52.

7. *Course in Miracles*, 275–79.

8. Karpinski, *Two Worlds*, 140, 238.

9. Fox, *Creation Spirituality*

10. Bruce, *Philippians*, 76.

11. Ralph P. Martin, *Philippians: A New Century Bible Commentary* (Grand Rapids, MI: Eerdmans, 1976), 154–55.

12. Bruce, *Philippians*, 125–26.

13. John R. W. Stott, *God's New Society: The Message of Ephesians* (Downers Grove, IL: InterVarsity, 1979), 131–34.

14. Houlden, *Paul's Letters*, 317–20.

15. Peter T. O'Brien, *The Epistle to the Philippians: A Commentary on the Greek Text* (Grand Rapids, MI: Eerdmans, 1991), 425–40.

16. Capra, *Uncommon Wisdom*, 67–70.

17. Markus Barth, *Ephesians 4–6: The Anchor Bible* (Garden City, NY: Doubleday, 1974), 543–45.

18. Pearce, *Magical Child Matures*, 186–87, 192–93.

19. Stott, *God's New Society*, 40, 80–83.

20. Talbot, *Beyond the Quantum*, 53–54.

21. Eduard Lohse, *Colossians and Philemon*, trans. William R. Poehlmann and Robert J. Karris (Philadelphia: Fortress, 1971), 46–50.

22. Fox, *Cosmic Christ*, 133–35.

23. Houlden, *Paul's Letters*, 277–78.

24. Markus Barth, *Ephesians 1–3: The Anchor Bible* (Garden City, NY: Doubleday, 1974), 205–8.

25. Capra, *Uncommon Wisdom*, 83–85, 141–43.

26. Morris Berman, *The Reenchantment of the World* (Ithaca, NY: Cornell University, 1981), 17–23, 69–70, 189, 233–34.

27. *Course in Miracles*, 272–75.

28. Spangler, *Revelation*, 117–19, 141–42.

29. John White, "Jesus, Evolution, and the Future of Humanity" in *Human Survival and Consciousness Evolution*, eds. Stanislav Grof and Marjorie L. Valier (Albany: State University of New York 1988), 125–28.

30. Lovelock, *Ages of Gaia*, 54, 63.

31. Ken Wilber, "Where It Was, There I Shall Become: Human Potentials and the Boundaries of the Soul" in *Beyond Health and Normality: Explorations of Exceptional Psychological Well-being*, eds. Roger Walsh and Dean H. Shapiro (New York: Van Nostrand, 1983), 108–9, 116.

32. Houlden, *Paul's Letters*, 304–5.

33. Bruce, *Philippians*, 39, 42.

34. Daniel Patte, *Paul's Faith and the Power of the Gospel* (Philadelphia: Fortress, 1983), 184–85.

35. Murray J. Harris, *Colossians and Philemon* (Grand Rapids, MI: Eerdmans, 1991), 196.

36. Fox, *Cosmic Christ*, 228–35.

37. Bruce, *Philippians*, 88, 93.

38. Warch, *New Thought*, 59.

39. Bohm, *Science, Order, and Creativity*, 240–71.

40. Keyes, *Higher Consciousness*, 42–43.

41. Streiker, *New Age Comes to Main Street*, 12.

CHAPTER **8**

Summary
and
Conclusions

TEACHINGS OF THE NEW AGE

In Chapter 2 the basic teachings of the New Age were summarized under eleven headings that I called principles. These were:

1. *Everything is divine, including human consciousness.*

2. *Truth is constituted from within.*

3. *Growth in consciousness or overcoming faulty consciousness is the key to blissful living and the immediate goal of all enlightened persons.*

TEACHINGS OF THE BIBLE

In light of our survey of selected books from Hebrew and Christian Scripture, it is possible to formulate eleven general biblical teachings that relate, by agreement or disagreement, with the eleven New Age principles. The Bible teaches that:

1. *God is the ultimate source of all else. The divine presence in all creation is especially discernible in human beings, including human consciousness. Humans resemble God by being made in God's image or by participation in the life of Christ.*

2. *Belief and thought affect truth found in one's life and world.*

3. *Growth in wisdom and overcoming faulty, faithless dispositions are the keys to blessedness and the immediate goals of all believers.*

4. *Death leads to reincarnation.*	**4.** *Death leads to resurrection.*
5. *There are numerous valid paths to divinity.*	**5.** *Loving and respecting all people, God invites everyone to blessedness through faith in the God of Israel, the God of Jesus Christ.*
6. *The attainment of bliss involves concern for the good of all.*	**6.** *The attainment of blessedness involves concern for the good of all.*
7. *Health means wholeness and unity of body, mind, and spirit.*	**7.** *Health means holiness in the unity of body, mind, and spirit.*
8. *The unity of all requires closeness to and respect for nature.*	**8.** *Human dominion over nature requires submission to God and sensitivity to God's presence in nature.*
9. *We need to trust intuition, imagination, and feeling.*	**9.** *Intuition, imagination, and feeling can be trustworthy elements of growth in faith.*
10. *We need to trust paranormal phenomena.*	**10.** *We can trust paranormal phenomena that befit a life of faith.*
11. *We need to trust the divine.*	**11.** *We need to trust God.*

These teachings, along with their corresponding New Age principles, can be compared and contrasted one pair at time.

1. Divinity and Grace

The New Age view of reality, seeing all as interrelated or one, surmises that consciousness is a necessary part of the totality.[1] Our survey of biblical literature shows how much the writers of Scripture connected consciousness with the life of faith and grace. But New Age monism, or belief in the divinity *of* all, differs from a biblical view whereby God is *in* all as a benevolent creator or whereby persons originally created in the image of God can additionally resemble God by grace. The differences between the Bible

and the New Age on this point seem to be among the most difficult to reconcile. Monism says each person, at least each growing
self, *is* God or the divine. The Bible says each person, in goodness
but not in sin, is *like* God. From the latter perspective, seeing God
as everything can appear as abhorrent as idolatrously identifying
God with a graven image.

Here the New Age seems to stand in marked contrast with the
Bible and with modern views that appreciate Eastern metaphysics
but which find absolute monistic or pantheistic views incomplete.[2]
But another New Age principle — the need for personal growth
and consciousness — suggests that individuals are often quite dis-
tanced from immediate and blissful oneness with the divine. That
is why growth in consciousness is necessary and wholesome.

One should perhaps observe as well that the monistic view of
"all as one," when coupled with the idea of maya or illusion, suggests in its own way how the divine is *in* what is perceived; for
"behind" or "in" the world of illusions, as seen by Eastern religions, is nothing other than the one that is divine. If the suggestion
holds, then both the monistic New Age view and the biblical view
perceive a unity in all things that also enjoy their kind of individuality. Both views would be acknowledging an illusory world or a
creation distinguishable from the divine or God and yet identified
with the divine or God within a single totality.

The commonality of visions, the accord that appears when
comparing heightened consciousness as a sense of universal oneness and as an experience of salvation as the Bible presents it, may
then rightly justify the application of the biblical term *grace* to a
cosmic sense of self [3] as understood in Eastern religions and the
New Age. In other words, the oneness of all, like the process of
salvation, is itself perceived as a kind of grace.

In contemporary physics, differing observations at the sub-
atomic level allow reality to appear alternately with both the indi-
viduating traits of particles and the unifying and communicative
traits of waves.[4] For the New Age such research discloses how
much reality, and thus the question of truth, is connected with the
perspectives one assumes. It may also show, as the Bible appears to
reveal, that distinctiveness and unity are complementary aspects of
a universe dependent on the divine.

Belief in growing toward or attaining salvation, the fullness of being, through the knowledge (*gnosis* in Greek) of one's divinity is a form of the centuries-old way of life called gnosticism. Such belief, with its close relationship to the biblical teachings on life in the Spirit, appears to have been one of many variant forms of belief during the earliest centuries of Christianity. Yet, in line with biblical views of likeness to God through faith, grace, and loving practice, gnosticism in its strict form of equating all human selfhood with God was condemned as a heresy. It is important however to remember that what gnosticism essentially has always striven for is transformation and perfection through the knowledge of God who lives within; the goal is thus to avoid distractions of nonessential externals.[5]

The epistle to the Ephesians appears to show great sensitivity to Gnosticism, but in a way that focuses first and foremost on the character of Christ rather than on the kind of divinity latent in all other persons.[6] This could well be seen as a source of traditional Christian doctrine connected with Christ's true divinity. In accord with such teaching, he alone can know himself as essentially God. Thus we might say that in these terms the only one who may legitimately act as a gnostic is Jesus. Such may well be suggested in Ephesians 4:13 where the Greek wording for Christ's "maturity" or mature manhood, terminology possibly influenced by Gnosticism, specifically designates perfect maleness, a fully developed individual personality. But as the "Perfect Man," he is the ideal of human perfection on whom all believers' full development or sanctity depends,[7] not someone who typifies what all humans essentially are.

By traditional Christian faith he *is* divine. Christians who believe in him are said to *share* in divinity by grace. Luke does not hesitate however to associate Jesus' development with grace or divine favor (Luke 2:40, 52)[8] in order to suggest the perfection of Jesus' growth.[9] This may help us conclude that Jesus' "gnosticism" was coupled with grace. Later gnostics who associated their sense of grace with a sense of their essential divinity were at least in good company even if by established Christian standards they were confused. In this light there may be more room for sympathy with gnosticism than is frequently the case.[10]

One may argue that New Age gnosticism entails a risk of confusing oneself with God and thus missing the benefits of belief in one's essential creatureliness.[11] Such argumentation does a service to the biblical views of creation and grace. But it also hinders an appreciation of gnosticism's honest quest for God and presumes that the mystery of all humanity's salvation is solved by clear-cut categories. Abuses that can indeed ensue from believing in àn ego-centered way that one is God can seemingly ensue with equal probability from an irresponsible persuasion that one is filled with divine grace.

From a different perspective both the New Age and the biblical views of oneness with the divine appear as ways of associating the face of God, divine goodness, with human persons and of challenging them to make the most of the goodness with which they and all creation are endowed. Both views call for recourse to the divine and for confidence in divine power to transform lives. Neither view wants to claim divinity for ego-centered or ungodly purposes. The Genesis account of Jacob's wrestling with God or God's agent at Jabbok is an extraordinary story depicting an extraordinary God.[12] For what kind of God would allow a mortal to overtake divinity? Perhaps a God who is strong enough, big enough, and loving enough to let the weaker seem for a time to win.

2. The Subject of Truth

The Bible and the New Age agree that subjective dispositions, namely the attitudes and perspectives of an individual, greatly determine what one experiences and how events in the individual's life transpire. Both views involve acceptance that positive thought allows one to experience greater harmony and peace in one's life and to have the kind of trust and tranquility that allow one best to influence a world often plagued by mistrust, disharmony, and disruption. The New Age view associates more power directly with the subject, or with the mind of the individual, since the self in higher consciousness naturally possesses divine power to influence and sustain desired outcomes. The Bible attributes absolute power to God alone but, by its beliefs in the effectiveness of speech and the tremendous power of prayer, finds that in their words and wishes believers have much more influence than they frequently dare to accept.

3. Self and Spirit

Both the Bible and the New Age see that negativity — in such forms as bitterness, resentment, and hate — hinders personal growth and deprives one of the happiness attainable by centering on the divine. Condemnation, ridicule, or control, says the New Age, flow from the unenlightened or ignorant ego that has strayed from its divine center or self.[13] Judging, mocking, or domineering, according to the Bible, flow from foolishness and sin, attachments to values that are not determined by the Spirit of God.

That is why the Bible and the New Age teach that forgiveness is one of the most powerful acts that a person can perform, and that the reconciliation that flows from forgiveness should lead to acceptance, kindness and love. Such virtues, says the New Age, can be part of a general heightening of consciousness, an expansion of thought and awareness on which, in an age of global crises of many kinds, the survival of ourselves and our planet may well depend.[14] The Bible sees such dispositions as part of the highest life of faith and the immediate outcome of a life guided by divine wisdom. For the New Age the immediate goal of higher consciousness is bliss or happiness.

4. Newness of Life

The ultimate goal of wisdom and higher consciousness is oneness with the divine. The Bible and the New Age understand such oneness differently as either full and permanent participation in God's heavenly life or as the full and permanent realization of one's divine self. The way to the former is through resurrection. The way to the latter is through reincarnation. The Bible's acceptance that the dead can appear to those living on earth reflects, along with Jewish anticipation of the return of such personalities as Elijah, belief in particular sorts of reincarnation.

But a closer parallel to reincarnation in the New Age sense appears to lie in the Biblical notion of resurrection as an entry into glorious bodily existence after a single biological death. Both kinds of ultimate transformation — resurrection and reincarnation — are forms of rebirth, renewal, or new life. In a broad sense then, reentry into a body, even a "spiritual" (I Corinthians 15:44) or risen body, can be called a reincarnation. Yet it is the multiplicity of earthly lives that distinguishes reincarnation in the strict sense from resurrection. Also, the New Age does not hold that reincarnation is permanently enduring because bodily existence ceases once a person has attained ultimate fullness as the divine.

Both forms of reincarnation, or rather, both reincarnation in the New Age sense and resurrection in the biblical sense allow those departed from earthly life to communicate with those still experiencing earthly life. For many New Agers, spiritualism is in its respectable forms a desirable way of receiving reliable guidance and for demonstrating belief in both the permanence of life and the illusory nature of death. From a biblical viewpoint, belief in resurrection causes death to lose its "sting" (I Cor 15:55).

Christians who believe in Purgatory hold that they may perform loving deeds of prayer and sacrifice for those departed who are thought to be possibly still developing toward a heavenly reward through purification and growth in the Spirit. Christians who believe in calling on all the holy ones — even those departed from this earth — for help through prayer can turn with devotion to the saints of heaven and ask for their intercession, along with Christ's, before the throne of God. From such perspectives both the Bible and the New Age recognize a solidarity between the living and the dead, either as members of Christ's body or as a community of benevolent spirits. In either case there is a vision of cooperation and fellowship as the universe, by grace or divine power, moves toward its ultimate fulfillment.

5. Universal Consciousness

The Bible is a collection of books specially designed to encourage a specific form of religiousness and devotion. Jews and Christians look to their Scripture, a work they regard as inspired, for direction in discerning what may belong and not belong to the faith by which they know their God. The wisdom they thus attain is for them a growing consciousness of God's universal love and God's desire for the unity of all humanity in righteousness and truth. The Bible is cautious, even restrictive, regarding religious beliefs and practices that are alien to such wisdom. Yet there appear to be in scriptural universalist perspectives at least a few glimpses of tolerance. Perhaps Paul captures something essential in the biblical disposition when he avers:

> *Indeed, even though there may be so-called gods in heaven or on earth*
> *— as in fact there are many gods and many lords — yet for us there is*
> *one God, the Father, from whom are all things and for whom we exist,*
> *and one LORD, Jesus Christ, through whom are all things and through*
> *whom we exist (I Cor 8:5–6).*

Next to the Bible, the New Age appears quite tolerant, perhaps even carefree regarding the appropriateness of a large number of religions, Western and Eastern, and a large number of practices, ancient and modern, for attaining higher consciousness and bliss. Here, according to the New Age, there need be no conflict between monism and monotheism, between belief that sees the divine as all and belief in a single and personal God above and in all; any way of sincerely honoring an aspect of the divine is seen as a way to honor God.[15] For the New Age only that which burdens consciousness, only that which tempts the ego away from the self is to be called an invalid path toward ultimate bliss and the unity of all in the divine. On this point the stated methodologies of the Bible and the New Age stand in notable contrast.

The objectives of both however appear to overlap considerably. With universal oneness and transformation as the goal, both stand together. New Agers can see biblical faith as part of the wondrous process.[16] Jews and Christians can respect the New Age similarly, if only to the extent that they can discern what of it belongs to the ways of God. Christians hearing their Lord say to those who wondered when they served him,

> *'Just as you did it to one of the least of these who are members of my*
> *family, you did it to me' (Mt 25:40b)*

can presume unbounded generosity and compassion in their Lord's presence to persons of goodwill.

6. Universal Love and Care

Differences in the area of global responsibility have more to do with metaphysics or philosophy than with practice. For both the Bible and the New Age all things are one, at least as interconnected. In terms of the implicate order appreciated by the New Age, all being is enfolded in unity at the deeper fundamental levels, and all persons are part of one consciousness. This consciousness appears remote or nonexistent when negative thought brings disharmony and turmoil between human beings. Entering deeply into one's own humanity however, which means experiencing oneness in a true love that surpasses mere sentiment, is to experience radically the universal order to which all are bound.[17] In the biblical view all falls under the Creator's providence or is harmonized in Christ who is the "firstborn" of creation. Responsible practice, involvement in the process of preserving and enhancing the status of all, is part of solidarity with God's universal graciousness. All sectors of society, all sectors of the environment, all nations, all races must be nurtured and transformed therefore by rightful and generous human love. Here the Bible and the New Age stand in utter agreement.

7. Total Health

The Bible and the New Age have little argument with one another respecting health. The interests of the body cannot be separated from the attitudes of the mind. And neither the mind nor the body subsists without the influence of the spirit by which one lives. The New Age views health and healing as the attainment of a wholeness, a completion of the work of harmonizing the elements of personal life. The Bible sees health as a blessing and a part of the holiness one attains by coordinating all aspects of one's life with the ways of God. In both views the coordination of body, mind, and spirit are essential. In both views this coordination is attained by drawing on the power of one's higher gifts. Thus the power of the self and the power of grace work to stimulate both wholeness and holiness.

8. Environmental Concern

The Bible rejoices in the beauty of creation, proclaims God's presence in all of nature, and enjoins on humanity a dominion over life on the earth. There is thus much room in a biblical view of creation for a sense of responsibility to the planet, and even the universe, which God has graciously produced. Such responsibility is grounded in and amplified by the biblical faith whereby all people enjoy God's benevolence and can attain greater unity in God's abundant grace. The New Age moves clearly in the direction of responsibility for peoples and the environment but offers far more specific guidelines for the effort. Here love of neighbor becomes inseparable from love of all creation.[18]

9. The Value of Imagery

New Age practice is frequently characterized by use of visualization and imagery to attain greater health, heightened consciousness, and holistic development. Imaging is part of recourse to the powers of the "right brain." Here the various elements of personal life can be drawn into harmony by giving them healthy contact with the unconscious. The imaginative play of a child works similarly.[19] In adults the imagination can lead to inner prompting or impulses that, if further freed into appropriate action, can be of great value to individuals and societies. Feelings elicited in this way, says the New Age, should be trusted.[20]

Biblical authors clearly knew the value of appealing to the imagination so that the human spirit, led by stories and pictures, could know the treasures of faith in God. Even Paul, whose theology is often weighty or abstract, regularly speaks in images, for example by calling the Christian community a "body" or "temple." Jesus was guiding the imagery of his listeners when he asked them to reflect on his parables and taught them by using earthy illustrations. He apparently knew that imagining such things as planting, harvesting, vineyards, fields, roads, merchants, rich people, and poor people can be part of awakening afresh to vibrant features of the Kingdom of God.

10. Paranormal Powers

The Bible speaks routinely and approvingly of divination, prophecy, faith healing, communication with the dead, telepathy, and psychokinesis. These are paranormal powers that are quite acceptable as part of the faith that the Bible proclaims, or as part of the work that God wants done. Such powers can be abused. They can be part of the devil's work. But so can anything of which the devil gets hold, including the words of Scripture (Luke 4:9–12). Like the Bible the New Age at times values synchronicity and paranormal powers as instruments of higher consciousness and as forces for improving the condition of the world. Charlatans are everywhere, and no less among devotees of the New Age. But the largely sincere and caring way in which the New Age employs such means should scarcely be doubted.

For both the Bible and the New Age, higher consciousness and whatever paranormal powers that attend it are ultimately designed for the spiritual unity of the divine and the human, not for personal grandeur alone. In the words of Paul:

> If I have prophetic powers, and understand all mysteries and all knowledge, and if I have all faith, so as to remove mountains, but do not have love, I am nothing (I Cor 13:2).

11. With Eyes Turned on High

The faith and love proclaimed by the Bible are intimately connected with hope. With minds and hearts turned toward God, believers can expect an abundance of divine assistance, consolation, support, and rewards. Such hope is the counterpart of obedience, the submission of oneself to the divine will in such a way that personal, free, and creative efforts are directed, sustained, and completed by God's grace. This assertive, hopeful, and obedient disposition is like Jacob's "victory" over God (Gn 32:28). Here God is overtaken. To live in hope means to exert one's own will and still trust God's.

The New Age lives in the same paradox of freedom and dependence. The petty ego must be voluntarily given up in favor of the fuller self.[21] Such submission requires setting one's vision higher than the limited parameters of the everyday world and trusting something greater and exceedingly more noble.[22] The character of this greater world transcending that of the human ego has been called divine[23] and so appears to be the reality that the Bible recognizes as a personal God. The contemporary physics to which the New Age turns for inspiration speculates that something like a universal mind, something traditionally called God, must be the power by which the multiplicity of conscious entities in the universe cohere in unity and order. For to see the regularity and patterns of nature as a series of chance events is blatantly to defy the laws of probability.[24]

Trust in the greater and higher, trust which is both creative and submissive, is a fundamental disposition for both the Bible and the New Age. Trust of this kind brings all the other principles, of both the Bible and the New Age movement, into due proportion and harmony. As a central feature of higher knowledge and awareness, trust so displayed allows the Bible and the New Age movement to appear as companions indeed, companions in consciousness with eyes turned on high.

FINAL THOUGHTS

The Bible and the New Age are notable sources of meaning and prominent guides to life. Between the Bible and the New Age there are differences. But by the reading of Scripture I have proposed and by the understanding of the New Age that I have set forth, there are also similarities. I conclude that between these two sources and guides there is much more kinship than division. Such a conclusion is admittedly controversial. It turns on an ability to see something of the hand of God, or something of divine power, in each of the "companions." The conclusion suggests that the proponents of each side of the dialogue can learn something of truth from one another. Neither side need, or probably can, accept *all* that the other has to say.

To focus on the Bible and the New Age as companions rather than competitors is to facilitate their attaining a concord that allows them to help, not hinder, one another in their respective aspirations and tasks. To hope for such companionship is to trust that it will happen, to await a more blessed and blissful future. Perhaps then New Agers will be helped to see more clearly where divine grace works in the world or where divinity becomes incarnated in human life. Perhaps then Jews and Christians will be helped to appreciate anew how wondrous activity, like the use of paranormal powers, can complement everyday empirical awareness. Perhaps then New Agers may better determine that whatever they might have found lacking in biblical faith was due to their limited perspectives. Perhaps then Jews and Christians may better understand that whatever might have attracted them to the New Age was already in their own backyards.

Notes

1. Capra, *Uncommon Wisdom*, 61.

2. Ken Wilber, *Eye to Eye: The Quest for the New Paradigm* (Boston: Shambhala, 1990), 152–59.

3. Spretnak, *States of Grace*, 24–27, 100, 113, 211.

4. Talbot, *Beyond the Quantum*, 18–27.

5. Morris Berman, *Coming to Our Senses* (New York: Simon & Schuster, 1989), 175–76.

6. Barth, *Ephesians 1–3*, 13–15.

7. Barth, *Ephesians 4–6*, 441, 484–97.

8. Raymond E. Brown, *The Birth of the Messiah: A Commentary on the Infancy Narratives in Matthew and Luke* (Garden City, NY: Doubleday, 1977), 483.

9. Marshall, *The Gospel of Luke*, 130.

10. Rossner, *The Primordial Tradition*, 122.

11. Peters, *Cosmic Self*, ix, 55–57, 130–31, 171, 182, 196.

12. Brueggemann, *Genesis*, 267.

13. *Course in Miracles*, 155–56, 244–45.

14. Roger Walsh, "Human Survival: A Psycho-Evolutionary Analysis" in *Human Survival and Consciousness Evolution*, eds. Stanislav Grof and Marjorie L. Valier (Albany: State University of New York, 1988), 2–3.

15. Carey, *Bird Tribes*, 139–40, 185–86.

16. Clancy, *New Age Guide*, 20.

17. Renée Weber, "The Enfolding-Unfolding Universe: A Conversation with David Bohm" in *The Holographic Paradigm and Other Paradoxes: Exploring the Leading Edge of Science*, ed. Ken Wilber (Boulder, CO: Shambhala, 1982), 72–77.

18. Wendell Berry, *The Gift of the Good Land: Further Essays Cultural and Agricultural* (San Francisco: North Point, 1981), 272–75.

19. Pearce, *Magical Child*, 144–45.

20. Roberts, *Individual and Mass Events*, 237–38, 244, 249, 294.

21. Karpinski, *Two Worlds*, 249–53.

22. *Course in Miracles*, 307–8.

23. Zukav, *Seat of the Soul*, 185–86.

24. Talbot, *Beyond the Quantum*, 193-98.

Works Cited

Baer, Randall N. and Vicki Vittitow Baer, *The Crystal Connection: A Guidebook for Personal and Planetary Ascension*. San Francisco: Harper, 1987.

Barth, Markus, *Ephesians 1–3: The Anchor Bible*. Garden City, NY: Doubleday, 1974.

Ephesians 4–6: The Anchor Bible. Garden City, NY: Doubleday, 1974.

Bateson, Gregory, *Mind and Nature: A Necessary Unity*. New York: Dutton, 1979.

Bateson, Gregory and Mary Catherine Bateson, *Angels Fear: Towards an Epistemology of the Sacred*. New York: Macmillan, 1987.

Bergant, Dianne, *What Are They Saying about Wisdom Literature?* New York: Paulist, 1984.

Berman, Morris, *Coming to Our Senses*. New York: Simon & Schuster, 1989.

The Reenchantment of the World. Ithaca, NY: Cornell University, 1981.

Berry, Wendell, *The Gift of the Good Land: Further Essays Cultural and Agricultural*. San Francisco: North Point, 1981.

Bohm, David and F. David Peat, *Science, Order, and Creativity*. New York: Bantam, 1987.

Boyd, Doug, *Mysteries, Magicians, and Medicine People: Tales of a Wanderer*. New York: Paragon House, 1989.

Brown, Raymond E., *The Birth of the Messiah: A Commentary on the Infancy Narratives in Matthew and Luke*. Garden City, NY: Doubleday, 1977.

Bruce, F.F., *Philippians: A Good News Commentary*. San Francisco: Harper, 1983.

Brueggemann, Walter, *Genesis*. Atlanta: John Knox, 1982.

The Message of the Psalms. Minneapolis: Augsburg, 1984.

Capra, Fritjof, *The Tao of Physics: An Exploration of the Parallels between Modern Physics and Eastern Mysticism*. New York: Bantam, 1977.

Uncommon Wisdom: Conversations with Remarkable People. New York: Simon & Schuster, 1988.

Carey, Ken, *Return of the Bird Tribes*. New York: Uni-Sun, 1988.

Terra Christa: The Global Spiritual Awakening. Kansas City: Uni-Sun, 1985.

Chandler, Russell and Marjorie Lee Chandler. "The Magnet of New Age Mysticism," *Columbia* (July 1990): 6–8.

Clancy, John et al., *A New Age Guide for the Thoroughly Confused and Absolutely Certain*. Eastsound, WA: Sweet Forever, 1988.

Clow, Barbara, "Reincarnation as Method for the Divine Quest," in *Fireball and the Lotus*, ed. Ron Miller and Jim Kenney, 228–248. Santa Fe, NM: Bear, 1987.

A Course in Miracles. Tiburon, CA: Foundation for Inner Peace, 1975.

Craigie, Peter C., *The Book of Deuteronomy*. Grand Rapids, MI: Eerdmans, 1976.

Dahood, Mitchell, *Psalms I. 1–50: The Anchor Bible*. Garden City, NY: Doubleday, 1966.

Psalms II. 51–100: The Anchor Bible. Garden City, NY: Doubleday, 1968.

Danker, Frederick W., *Jesus and the New Age. A Commentary on St. Luke's Gospel*. Philadelphia: Fortress, 1988.

Dauber, Kenneth, "The Bible as Literature: Reading Like the Rabbis," *Semeia* 31 (1985): 27–48.

Dowd, Alice, "The 'New Age' for Libraries," *Library Journal* 114 (July 1989): 44–50.

"What's New in the New Age," *Library Journal* 116 (March 15, 1991): 58–61.

Dyrness, William, "Stewardship of the Earth in the Old Testament," in *Tending the Garden: Essays on the Gospel and the Earth*, ed. Wesley Granberg-Michaelson. Grand Rapids, MI: Eerdmans, 1986, 50–65.

Edwards, Jr., O.C., *Luke's Story of Jesus*. Philadelphia: Fortress, 1981.

Eichrodt, Walter, *Theology of the Old Testament*, Vol. 1., trans. J. A. Baker. Philadelphia: Westminster, 1961.

English-Lueck, J.A., *Health in the New Age: A Study in California Holistic Practices*. Albuquerque: University of New Mexico, 1990.

Ferguson, Marilyn, *The Aquarian Conspiracy: Personal and Social Transformation in the 1980s*. Los Angeles: Tarcher, 1980.

"Karl Pribram's Changing Reality," in *The Holographic Paradigm and Other Paradoxes: Exploring the Leading Edge of Science*, ed. Ken Wilber. Boston: Shambhala, 1982, 15–26.

The Fireside Treasury of Light, ed. Mary Olsen Kelly. New York: Simon & Schuster, 1990.

Fisch, Harold, *Poetry with a Purpose: Biblical Poetics and Interpretation.* Bloomington, IN: Indiana University, 1988.

Fitzmyer, Joseph A., *The Gospel according to Luke. I–IX: The Anchor Bible.* Garden City, NY: Doubleday, 1981.

The Gospel according to Luke. X–XXIV: The Anchor Bible. Garden City, NY: Doubleday, 1985.

Fox, Matthew, *The Coming of the Cosmic Christ: The Healing of Mother Earth and the Birth of a Global Renaissance.* San Francisco: Harper, 1988.

Creation Spirituality: Liberating Gifts for the Peoples of the Earth. San Francisco: Harper, 1991.

Gooding, David, *According to Luke: A New Exposition of the Third Gospel.* Grand Rapids, MI: Eerdmans, 1987.

Grof, Christina and Stanislav Grof, *The Stormy Search for Self: A Guide to Personal Growth through Transformational Crises.* Los Angeles: Tarcher, 1990.

Groothuis, Douglas R., *Unmasking the New Age.* Downers Grove, IL: InterVarsity, 1986.

Harris, Murray J., *Colossians and Philemon.* Grand Rapids, MI: Eerdmans, 1991.

Heaney, John J., *The Sacred and the Psychic: Parapsychology and Christian Theology.* New York: Paulist, 1984.

Houlden, J. L., *Paul's Letters from Prison: Philippians, Colossians, Philemon, and Ephesians.* Philadelphia: Westminster, 1970.

Humphreys, W. Lee., *Joseph and His Family: A Literary Study*. Columbia, SC: University of South Carolina, 1988.

Joy, W. Brugh, "A Heretic in a New Age Community," in *Meeting the Shadow: The Hidden Power of the Dark Side of Human Nature*, eds. Jeremiah Abrams and Connie Zweig. Los Angeles: Tarcher, 1991, 150–52.

Jung, C. G., *Memories, Dreams, Reflections*, trans. Richard and Clara Winston. New York: Vintage, 1989.

Justice, Blair, *Who Gets Sick: How Beliefs, Moods and Thoughts Affect Your Health*. Los Angeles: Tarcher, 1988.

Karpinski, Gloria D., *Where Two Worlds Touch: Spiritual Rites of Passage*. New York: Ballantine, 1990.

Keyes, Ken, Jr., *Handbook to Higher Consciousness*. Coos Bay, OR: Love Line, 1975.

Kraus, Hans–Joachim, *Psalms 1–59: A Commentary*, trans. Hilton C. Oswald. Minneapolis: Augsburg, 1988.

   Psalms 60–150, trans. Hilton C. Oswald. Minneapolis: Augsburg, 1989.

   Theology of the Psalms, trans. Keith Crim. Minneapolis: Augsburg, 1986.

Krentz, Edgar, *The Historical-Critical Method*. Philadelphia: Fortress, 1975.

Lohse, Eduard, *Colossians and Philemon*, trans. William R. Poehlmann and Robert J. Karris. Philadelphia: Fortress, 1971.

Lovelock, James, *The Ages of Gaia: A Biography of Our Living Earth*. New York: Norton, 1988.

Marshall, I. Howard, *The Gospel of Luke: A Commentary on the Greek Text*. Grand Rapids, MI: Eerdmans, 1978.

Martin, Ralph P., *Philippians: A New Century Bible Commentary*. Grands Rapids, MI: Eerdmans, 1976.

McKane, William, *Proverbs: A New Approach*. Philadelphia: Westminster, 1970.

McKenzie, John L., *A Theology of the Old Testament*. Garden City, NY: Doubleday, 1974.

McKnight, Edgar V., *Post-modern Use of the Bible: The Emergence of Reader-oriented Criticism*. Nashville: Abingdon, 1988.

McRoberts, Kerry D., *New Age or Old Lie?* Peabody, MA: Hendrickson, 1989.

Melton, J. Gordon et al., *New Age Almanac*. New York: Visible Ink, 1991.

New Age Encyclopedia. Detroit: Gale Research, 1990.

Meye, Robert P., "Invitation to Wonder: Toward a Theology of Nature," in *Tending the Garden: Essays on the Gospel and the Earth*, ed. Wesley Granberg-Michaelson. Grand Rapids, MI: Eerdmans, 1986, 30–49.

Murphy, Roland E., *The Tree of Life: An Exploration of Biblical Wisdom Literature*. New York: Doubleday, 1990.

The New Age Dictionary: A Guide to Planetary Consciousness, ed. Alex Jack. Tokyo: Japan Publications, 1990.

Not Necessarily the New Age: Critical Essays. ed. Robert Basil. Buffalo, NY: Prometheus, 1988.

O'Brien, Peter T., *The Epistle to the Philippians: A Commentary on the Greek Text*. Grand Rapids, MI: Eerdmans, 1991.

Patte, Daniel, *Paul's Faith and the Power of the Gospel*. Philadelphia: Fortress, 1983.

Pearce, Joseph Chilton, *The Crack in the Cosmic Egg*. New York: Julian, 1971.

Magical Child Matures. New York: Dutton, 1985.

Magical Child: Rediscovering Nature's Plan for Our Children. New York: Dutton, 1977.

Peretti, Frank E., *This Present Darkness.* Westchester, IL: Crossway, 1986.

Pervo, Richard I., *Profit with Delight: The Literary Genre of the Acts of the Apostles.* Philadelphia: Fortress, 1987.

Peters, Ted, *The Cosmic Self: A Penetrating Look at Today's New Age Movements.* San Francisco: Harper, 1991.

Pollack, Detlef. "Vom Tischrücken zur Psychodynamik: Formen ausserkirchlicher Religiosität in Deutschland," *Schweizerische Zeitschrift für Soziologie/Revue Suisse de sociologie* 16, no. 1 (November 1990): 107–34.

Polzin, Robert, *Samuel and the Deuteronomist: A Literary Study of the Deuteronomic History. Part Two, I Samuel.* San Francisco: Harper, 1989.

Ram Dass, *Grist for the Mill.* New York: Bantam, 1981.

Rath, Ralph, *The New Age: A Christian Critique.* South Bend, IN: Greenlawn, 1990.

Rea, John D., *Healing and Quartz Crystals: A Journey with Our Souls.* Boulder, CO: Two Trees, 1986.

Roberts, Jane, *The Individual and the Nature of Mass Events.* New York: Prentice Hall, 1981.

Rossner, John, *In Search of the Primordial Tradition and the Cosmic Christ.* St. Paul, MN: Llewellyn, 1989.

Russell, Peter, *The Global Brain: Speculations on the Evolutionary Leap to Planetary Consciousness.* Los Angeles: Tarcher, 1983.

Schorsch, Christof, "Utopie und Mythos der Neuen Zeit: zur Problematik des 'New Age'," *Theologische Rundshau* 5 (1989): 315–30.

Shapiro, Dean H., Jr., "A Content Analysis of Eastern and Western Approaches to Therapy, Health, and Healing," in *Beyond Health and Normality: Explorations of Exceptional Psychological Well-being*, ed. Roger N. Walsh and Dean H. Shapiro, Jr.. New York: Van Nostrand, 1983, 433–91.

Siegel, Bernie S., *Peace, Love and Healing: Bodymind Communication and the Path to Self-Healing: An Exploration*. New York: Harper, 1989.

Skehan, Patrick W. and Alexander A. Di Lella, *The Wisdom of Ben Sira: The Anchor Bible*. New York: Doubleday, 1987.

Snaith, John G., *Ecclesiasticus or The Wisdom of Jesus Son of Sirach*. Cambridge: Cambridge University, 1974.

Spangler, David, *Emergence: The Rebirth of the Sacred*. New York: Dell, 1984.

Revelation: The Birth of a New Age. San Francisco: Rainbow Bridge, 1976.

Spretnak, Charlene, *The Spiritual Dimension of Green Politics*. Santa Fe, NM: Bear, 1986.

States of Grace: The Recovery of Meaning in the Postmodern Age. San Francisco: Harper, 1991.

Spretnak, Charlene and Fritjof Capra, *Green Politics*. Santa Fe, NM: Bear, 1986.

Stott, John R. W., *God's New Society: The Message of Ephesians*. Downers Grove, IL: InterVarsity, 1979.

Strauss, Leo, "The Beginnings of the Bible and Its Greek Counterparts," in *Genesis: Modern Critical Interpretations*, ed. Harold Bloom. New York: Chelsea, 1986, 23–42.

Streiker, Lowell D., *New Age Comes to Main Street: A Non-Hysterical Survey of the New Age Movement*. Nashville: Abingdon, 1990.

Talbot, Michael, *Beyond the Quantum*. New York: Macmillan, 1986.

Tarcher, Jeremy, "New Age as Perennial Philosophy," *New Realities* (May–June 1988): 27–28.

Teilhard de Chardin, Pierre, *The Future of Man*, trans. Norman Denny. New York: Harper, 1964.

Toolan, David, *Facing West from California's Shores: A Jesuit's Journey into New Age Consciousness*. New York: Crossroad, 1987.

Vaughan, Frances, *The Inward Arc: Healing and Wholeness in Psychotherapy and Spirituality*. Boston: Shambhala, 1986.

Vawter, Bruce, *On Genesis: A New Reading*. Garden City, NY: Doubleday, 1977.

Villoldo, Alberto and Stanley Krippner, *Healing States*. New York: Simon & Schuster, 1986.

von Rad, Gerhard, *Deuteronomy: A Commentary*. Philadelphia: Westminster, 1966.

Genesis: A Commentary. Philadelphia: Westminster, 1972.

Old Testament Theology, Vol. 1. New York: Harper, 1962.

Walsh, Roger N., "Human Survival: A Psycho-Evolutionary Analysis," in *Human Survival and Consciousness Evolution*, ed. Stanislav Grof and Marjorie L. Valier. Albany: State University of New York, 1988, 1–8.

The Spirit of Shamanism. Los Angeles: Tarcher, 1990.

Warch, William, *The New Thought Christian*. Marina del Rey, CA: DeVorss, 1977.

Weber, Renée, "The Enfolding-Unfolding Universe: A Conversation with David Bohm," in *The Holographic Paradigm and Other Paradoxes: Exploring the Leading Edge of Science*, ed. Ken Wilber. Boston: Shambhala, 1982, 44–104.

Westermann, Claus, *Genesis 12–36: A Commentary*, trans. John J. Scullion. Minneapolis: Augsburg, 1985.

Genesis 37–50: A Commentary, trans. John J. Scullion. Minneapolis: Augsburg, 1986.

White, John, "Enlightenment and the Christian Tradition," in *What Is Enlightenment?*, ed. John White. Los Angeles: Tarcher, 1984, 122–29.

"Jesus, Evolution, and the Future of Humanity," in *Human Survival and Consciousness Evolution* ed.Stanislav Grof and Marjorie L. Valier. Albany: State University of New York, 1988, 119–34.

Wilber, Ken, *Eye to Eye: The Quest for the New Paradigm*. Boston: Shambhala, 1990.

No Boundary: Eastern and Western Approaches to Personal Growth. Boston: Shambhala, 1979.

"Two Modes of Knowing," in *Beyond Ego: Transpersonal Dimensions in Psychology*, ed. Roger N. Walsh and Frances Vaughan. Los Angeles: Tarcher, 1980, 234–40.

"Where It Was, There I Shall Become: Human Potentials and the Boundaries of the Soul," in *Beyond Health and Normality: Explorations of Exceptional Psychological Well-being*, ed. Roger N. Walsh and Dean H. Shapiro, Jr. New York: Van Nostrand, 1983, 67–121.

Wilkinson, Loren, "New Age, New Consciousness and the New Creation," in *Tending the Garden: Essays on the Gospel and the Earth*, ed. Wesley Granberg-Michaelson. Grand Rapids, MI: Eerdmans, 1986, 6–29.

Wolf, Fred Alan, *Parallel Universes: The Search for Other Worlds*. New York: Simon & Schuster, 1990.

Zukav, Gary, *The Seat of the Soul*. New York: Simon & Schuster, 1989.

Scriptural Index

The pages of the book are in parentheses.

Subject Index

185

About the Author

RONALD QUILLO has been active in higher education and parish ministry since 1968. As a faculty member at several colleges and universities, he has contributed to the education of women and men for various helping professions, including psychology, nursing, and social work. His specialization, however, has been preparing students for ministry. In 1992 he assumed the position of professor of Systematics and Spirituality at the Oblate School of Theology in San Antonio, Texas.

Originally from St. Louis, he holds a Master of Arts degree in philosophy from De Paul University in Chicago, a Licentiate in Theology from the Catholic Institute of Paris, France, and a Doctorate in Theology from the University of Münster in Germany. He has also done postdoctoral studies in psychology at Spalding University in Louisville. His recent articles are directed toward holistic education and the psychological interpretation of Scripture. He was elected to serve as president of the scholastic honors society, Delta Epsilon Sigma for the 1992–1994 term.

Enriched by the challenges of family life, he enjoys partnering with his wife in the support and encouragement of six children, who have attained or are close to college age.